D1180230

CATHOLIC ANSWERS CLASSICS

The Third Day

Arnold Lunn

The Third Day

Catholic Answers Press

The Third Day was originally published in 1945 by the Newman Book Shop, Westminster, Maryland. This 2014 edition by Catholic Answers Press includes minor revisions.

©2014 Catholic Answers Press

Biblical references in this book are taken from the Catholic Edition of the Revised Standard Version of the Bible, © 1965, 1966 by the Division of Christian Education of the National Council of the Churches of Christ in the United States of America. Used by permission. All rights reserved.

Except for quotations, no part of this book may be reproduced or transmitted in any form or by any means, electronic or mechanical, including photocopying, recording, uploading to the Internet, or by any information storage and retrieval system, without written permission from the publisher.

Nihil obstat: Edward A. Cerny, S.S., D.D., *Censor Librorum*
Imprimatur: Michael J. Curly, D.D., Archbishop of Baltimore and Washington

Published by Catholic Answers, Inc.
2020 Gillespie Way
El Cajon, California 92020
888-291-8000 orders
619-387-0042 fax
www.catholic.com

Printed in the United States of America

ISBN 978-1-938983-78-8

Cover design by Devin Schadt
Typesetting by Nora Malone

TO MY WIFE

Uxor vivamus ut viximus et teneamus
   nomina quae primo sumpsimus in thalamo;
nec ferat ulla dies, ut commutemur in aevo,
   quin tibi sim juvenis tuque puella mihi.
Nestore sim quamvis provectior aemulaque annis
   vincas Cumanam tu quoque Deiphoben,
nos ignoremus quid sit matura senectus,
   scire aevi mentum, non numerare decet.

Contents

Introduction

MY FATHER, THE LATE Sir Henry Lunn, was a devout Methodist and a lifelong Liberal. Shortly before his death in March 1939, he said to me: "When I was a young man, life was very simple. One went to a political meeting and looked at the hats outside. The big hats were the hats of Liberals because Liberals have big brains. The small hats were the hats of Conservatives, with their stupid loyalty to the *status quo*. One does not need brains to stand still. In those days continental Liberals, groaning beneath foreign tyrants, looked to us for help and encouragement. Garibaldi in Italy and Kossuth in Hungary asked for nothing better than to wrest a constitution, patterned on ours, from the autocratic rulers of their countries. When Garibaldi set out from Sicily, the Cabinet sent him a book on the British

Constitution. You think that funny. So do I—now. But I didn't then, for London was then the spiritual capital of Liberalism just as Rome is of Roman Catholicism. In those days, 'to be young was very heaven,' provided that you were a young Liberal. I was confident that the extension of the franchise and of educational facilities and free trade and the universal adoption of the British Parliamentary system would solve all the major problems both of war and of peace, and usher in a new era of peace and social justice."

He paused and added sadly, "I have lived on, as an old man, to see country after country repudiating with disgust Parliamentary democracy, and the tyrannies and brutalities of a pagan world returning to an enslaved Europe."

The irrelevance of religion was the great heresy of the nineteenth century. Many good Christians believed, as my father certainly believed, that the moral standards that Christianity had imposed on the world would survive the repudiation of the Christian creed. We who have watched the tragic experiment of national apostasy in two great European countries—Russia, which officially adopted atheism as her state philosophy, and Germany, where the Nazis strove to substitute the worship of race for the worship of Christ—have no excuse for illusions. We know that *it does* matter what a man believes.

My father was not wholly uninfluenced by the prevailing belief that religion was essentially an individual matter. He looked to the churches to make men good, and to the state to make them happy, and was convinced that Liberalism was the key to our secular problems in this world, and a reunited Church to the problems of the world to come. He certainly did not realize that all our controversies are, as Cardinal Manning somewhere says, primarily theological, that the English way of life has its roots in the Christian faith, and that the nobler ideals of Liberalism were a byproduct of the Christianity that many Liberals had already repudiated.

My father was a great student of ancient and modern history, and, though uninterested in art, he was not unaware of certain aspects of that cultural decline which always coincides with a religious decline, but being an incurable optimist, he would have allowed the appeal from facts to faith and given his verdict against that great scientist and Nobel Prize winner, the late Alexis Carrel.

"The supremacy of matter and the dogmas of industrial religion," writes Carrel, "have destroyed culture, beauty, and morals, as they were understood by the Christian civilization, mother of modern science. Unintelligence is becoming more and more general in spite of the excellence of the courses given in the schools, colleges, and universities. Strange to say it often exists with advanced scientific knowledge. Moral sense is almost completely ignored by modern society. We have, in fact, suppressed its manifestations."

The flight from faith, the flight from morals, and the flight from beauty are coincident phenomena.

"Today," adds Alexis Carrel, who was an American of French background, "France despises the majestic remnants of her past and even destroys her natural beauties. The descendants of the men who conceived and erected the monastery of Mount Saint-Michel no longer understand its splendour. They cheerfully accept the indescribable ugliness of the modern houses in Normandy and Brittany, and especially in the Paris suburbs. Like Mount Saint-Michel and the majority of the French cities and villages, Paris has been disgraced by a hideous commercialism. During the history of a civilization, *the sense of beauty, like moral sense,* grows, reaches its optimum, declines, and disappears" (italics mine).

The great culture of Christendom was born, as every great culture was born, in an age of faith. The art, architecture, and literature of the great centuries were the outcome of an attempt to translate into paint, stone, or words the vision of eternal beauty and timeless truth.

We are living today in the winter of our Western civilization. Faith has been eroded by skepticism, and though works of beauty are still being produced, creative genius finds expression not in art but in engineering achievements. The age of nihilism can only destroy the legacy of beauty we have inherited from the age of faith. "We can learn all we wish to know," writes the greatest non-Christian philosopher of modern times, Oswald Spengler,

> about the art-clamour which a megalopolis sets up in order to forget that its art is dead from the Alexandria of the year 200. There, as here in our

world cities, we find a pursuit of illusions of artistic progress, of personal peculiarity, of "the new style," of "unsuspected possibilities," theoretical babble, pretentious fashionable artists . . . the unabashed farce of Expressionism. . . . Alexandria, too, had problem-dramatists and box-office artists whom it preferred to Sophocles, and painters who invented new tendencies and successfully bluffed their public. What do we possess today as "art"? A faked music, filled with artificial noisiness of massed instruments; a faked painting, full of idiotic, exotic, and showcard effects, that every ten years or so concocts out of the form-wealth of millennia some new "style," which is, in fact, no style at all, since everyone does as he pleases; a lying plastic that steals from Assyria, Egypt, and Mexico indifferently.

It is not only art that declines as religion declines but also compassion. "Cruelty and the abuse of power," wrote Dickens, "are the twin bad passions of human nature." Now, men did not cease to be cruel and tyrannical merely because they were baptized, but the compassion of Christ armored the merciful with the supreme argument for mercy. Christians were alternately incited to reform by the appeal of saints and goaded into reform by the taunts of skeptics, for there was no answer to the contrast between the compassion that Christ preached and the cruelties that Christians practiced. Slowly Catholics ceased to burn Protestants in Spain, and Protestants ceased to rack and hang Catholics in England, but all these hard-won gains of the Christian spirit have been lost in the countries whose rulers have explicitly or implicitly repudiated Christianity. One has only to contrast the worst atrocities proved, or alleged, against the Kaiser's Germany with the torture chambers of the Gestapo, in Paris, and elsewhere, to realize the tragic consequences of apostasy.

Men fought bravely before Christ was born, and heroism will continue to flower on the battlefields, even though the Church returns to the catacombs, but the whole nature of war will be transformed for the worse if the flight from Christianity is not arrested.

In his "Life" of the great Duke of Marlborough, Mr. Churchill quotes a royal proclamation at the outbreak of the war in 1702 to the effect that enemy subjects "who shall demean themselves dutifully to us shall be safe in their persons and estates." Mr. Churchill adds, "This passage will jar on the modern mind. We see how strong was the structure of Christendom in those times, and with what restraints even warring nations acted. Of course, nowadays, with the many improvements that have been made in international morals and behaviour, all enemy subjects—as in every other state based on an educated democracy—would be treated within twenty-four hours as malignant foes, flung into internment camps, and their private property stolen to assist the expenses of war. In the twentieth century mankind has shaken itself free from all those illogical, old-world prejudices, and achieved the highest efficiency of brutal, ruthless war."

And Mr. Churchill proceeds to give other instances of the "archaic doctrine" that was accepted as self-evident when "the structure of Christendom" was still unimpaired: the inevitable armistice at the end of battle to rescue the wounded, "instead of leaving them to perish inch by inch in agony in No Man's Land," the courtesies extended to the enemy passports to traverse hostile territory, ". . . no hatred, apart from military antagonism was countenanced . . . mob violence and mechanical propaganda had not yet been admitted to the adjustments of International disputes."

The French Revolution initiated the new age, for the revolution was a revolt not only against the nobility but also against Christianity, a revolt in the course of which, as Burke complains, the Jacobins destroyed "that mode of civilised war which, more than anything else, has distinguished the Christian religion."

One need not be a Christian to realize the relation ship between religion and morals. There is nothing new in that decline of morality and common honesty that the late Archbishop of Canterbury so often deplored. Polybius, the Greek historian, was a skeptic, but he was an intelligent skeptic, and his explanation of Greek dishonesty was similar to that advanced by Archbishop Temple.

"The Romans," said Polybius, "were more honest than the Greeks because of their scrupulous fear of the gods. It was therefore not without purpose or at random that our forefathers introduced among the common people those beliefs about gods and the punishments in Hades. Indeed, I think that men nowadays are very foolish and rash to reject them. And it is for this reason that Greek statesmen, if entrusted with a single talent, though protected by ten checking-clerks, ten seals and twenty witnesses, cannot be induced to keep faith; whereas, among the Romans, men of their magistracies and embassies are entrusted with large sums of money, and keep faith from pure respect of their oaths."

It is not only honesty and morality that decline as religion declines. If man is nothing more than first cousin to the chimpanzee, he has no logical ground of complaint if he is put behind bars. "Christianity," as Mr. Walter Lippmann reminds us, "anchored the rights of man in the structure of the universe. It set those rights where they were apart from human interference. Thus the pretensions of despots became heretical. And since that Revelation, though many despots have had the blessings of the clergy, no tyranny has possessed a clear title before the tribunal of the human conscience, no slave has had to feel that the hope of freedom was for ever closed. For in the recognition that there is in each man a final essence—that is, an immortal soul—which only God can judge, a limit was set upon the dominion of men over men." And it is, as Mr. Lippmann insists, no accident that "the only open challenge to the totalitarian state has come from men of deep religious faith."

But as "deep religious faith" declines, slavery returns. The repudiation of one "in whose service is perfect freedom" inevitably leads to the Tyrant State. There can be no collective security without collective Christianity.

Nothing but a religious revival, of which for the moment there is little evidence, can reintegrate a dying civilization born, as all great civilizations have been born, in an age of faith, for the end of atheism is death. When men cease to believe in God, they cease to believe in themselves. When religion dies, man loses his belief in the significance of life and, too bored to reproduce himself, lies down to die amid the mechanical marvels of a materialistic civilization. Every great culture begins, as Spengler says, with a strong affirmation of life and ends with a metaphysical turning toward death. "Children do not happen, not because children have become impossible, but principally because intelligence at the peak of intensity can no longer find any reason for their existence."

Spengler was a determinist. He offered us only the consolation of *understanding* the inevitable decline of our Western civilization, but to the Christian there are no irreversible tendencies. Courage and faith in England saved us in 1940. Courage and faith in Christ may yet prove Spengler a false prophet.

II

In the spring of 1944, I was invited to address a group of undergraduates of London University, and I chose for my theme the bankruptcy of secularism. I have reproduced the substance of my talk in the preceding pages. When I had finished, my friend and chairman, Dr. C.E.M. Joad, said: "We have listened to a profoundly depressing talk, but I don't find it easy to refute Lunn's thesis." After the lecture, Joad said to me, "You formulated thoughts which I have carefully kept at the back of my mind for some time, and which I was reluctant to admit."

The undergraduates took me up on minor points, but there was little attempt to dispute the main thesis. One of them came up to me at the end of the meeting and said that if I had given the same talk before the war, I would have met with lively opposition, but that most of them felt rather at sea and had nothing positive to fall back on.

The truth is that the Nazi-Russian pact and the attack on Finland shattered the faith of the few genuine idealists who had sought in Marxism a substitute for religion. Whereas in the nineties many intelligent people were convinced that Christianity was dying, and that the attack of so-called scientific materialism was irresistible, today it is the heresies of the nineteenth century that are on their deathbed. Materialism was like a vicious dog, and its bite was painful, but "the dog it was that died."

The great heresy of the nineteenth century that infected even good Christians like my father was the belief in the inevitability of progress. "Progress," wrote Herbert Spencer, "is not an accident but a necessity. What we call evil and immorality must disappear. It is certain that man must become perfect." "Viewed from Mount Vernon Street," writes Henry Adams of Boston society in 1848, "the problem of life was as simple as it was classic. Politics offered no difficulties, for there the moral law was a sure guide. Social perfection was also sure, because human nature worked for Good, and three instruments were all she asked—Suffrage, Common Schools, and the Press. On these points doubt was forbidden. Education was divine, and man needed only a correct knowledge of facts to reach perfection. Nothing quieted doubt so completely as the mental calm of the Unitarian clergy."

My father, as I have shown, was inclined to believe that Parliamentary democracy, compulsory education, and free trade would solve all *secular* difficulties, leaving the Church to provide spiritual remedies for spiritual diseases. If the world had steadily improved in proportion as Christianity declined, the task of the Christian apologist would be difficult, but as the exact reverse is the case, the Christian can, at least, console himself with the reflection that whereas the secular optimism of the nineteenth century has been refuted by events, the realism of Christianity has been vindicated by history. Ours is a philosophy that *explains* history, and, come what may, we can say with Clough, "It fortifies my soul to know / That though I perish truth is so."

Or, as the great eighteenth-century Anglican Bishop Butler said: "Things are what they are, and the consequences will be what they will be. Why then should we deceive ourselves?"

The confident "Dawnism" of the nineteenth century has given way to disillusion. Even before this war, Mr. Belloc noted, as one of the characteristics of the modern world, the rising tide of despair.

And therein lies our opportunity. The rival philosophies have been exposed for the shoddy substitutes that they are, but one great obstacle to a Christian revival still remains to be overcome: the traditional reluctance of ninety-nine Christians out of a hundred to make the slightest effort to convert their non-Christian neighbors.

Most of those who yield, as every Christian must yield at least nominal assent to the belief that Christianity is the most important of all beliefs, habitually act on the assumption that it is an irrelevance with no real influence on the practical business of life. Even good Christians behave as if they believed that the maladies of this distracted planet are due to political rather than to religious causes.

The defense of Christianity is left to the priests and to a few eccentric laymen, regarded with good-humored amusement by most of their fellow Christians, but the defense of our political panaceas is assumed to be the business of Mr. Everyman. As elections approach, thousands of good Christians, who would be horrified at the suggestion that they should canvass for Christ, will canvass with great enthusiasm for the political party of their choice. "Nobody is ever converted by argument" is a formula as popular with Christians as it is unknown among politicians and political canvassers.

There is an increasing tendency among Christians to forget that a just social order is a byproduct of a Christian society and that it is vain to hope for the byproducts once we have lost the thing itself. We must, of course, continue to work for social justice, but we must not confuse political panaceas, which are, at best, drugs to alleviate the pain, with that organic treatment of the disease which is involved in the Christianization of society. It is a question not of competition but of priorities. We must put first things first, instead of relegating apologetics to a very secondary position, for if there is no return to Christianity, it is certain that our society will perish. "There will always be an England," provided and provided only that England is reconverted to Christianity. If not, our "finest hour" in 1940 will also prove to be our sunset hour.

III

Many years ago, I was asked to read a document that purported to describe the circumstances under which a Jesuit mission in South America had buried gold and precious stones of fabulous value. An enterprising and plausible gentleman had invited two friends of mine to invest money in a company formed to hunt for this buried treasure and to join the expedition that was being organized for this purpose. My advice was asked, and I gave it as my opinion that the document was a fake. One of my friends took my advice. The other invested his money and was repaid in the dividend of adventure, the adventure incidental to the search for nonexistent treasure in the remote regions of South America.

I often recall the passionate intensity with which we debated the authenticity of this document, for there are few things people will examine with greater care than a project that promises to make their fortune. Cynics have asserted that there is no more searching test of the genuineness of a man's beliefs than his readiness to invest money in support of them. Political questions interest us because they touch our pocket. We are all amateur doctors because health means even more to us than wealth, and a man who claimed to know of a cure for the common cold would be listened to with eager attention and blamed if he did not propagate his recipe among his friends. Christians are alleged to value spiritual health above physical health, and there are some who do, but most of us are paralyzed by shyness in our approach to those who are suffering from something more serious than the common cold. If Christianity is true, we have the key not only to eternal happiness in the world to come but also to the secular maladies of this distracted planet, but do we *act* as if we believed that we alone possessed the one sovereign remedy for the disorders of the world?

If I were convinced that I found the cure for cancer, I would master the evidence in favor of the cure and propagate my knowledge by all means in my power, but most Christians might be compared to a man who, knowing a cure for cancer, thought it indecent to mention the fact to a friend dying of the disease, but rational to spend hours arguing the merits of the Beveridge cold cure, or the "New Deal" headache pills.

The collapse of moral standards is causing such concern that proposals are being discussed to improve the religious education in our secondary and elementary schools, but the revolt against dogma has gone so far that it is more than probable that Christianity will be represented as nothing more than humanitarianism flavored by religiosity. "La religiosità è vaga," said Croce, "la religione è precisa." Religiosity is vague, religion is precise, and it is only the precision of traditional Christianity that can save us.

Religious education should begin with the New Testament. Is the New Testament fact or fiction? Was St. Luke written by St. Luke or by some second-century forger? Precise questions that the prophets of religiosity may be forgiven for evading but which should be faced and discussed in any scheme of Christian education.

Testament means "will," and the first thing we do to a will is prove it. Can we prove that the New Testament is what it purports to be—God's legacy to man?

I am not, of course, suggesting that the authenticity of the Gospels could ever provoke among normal people the same intense interest as the authenticity of a document purporting to describe the location of buried treasure in South America. I have not forgotten the first principle of all good advocacy: moderation. *Est modus in rebus*, but I am rash enough to suppose that an odd hour or two at the end of a boy's school life might not be unprofitably spent in armoring him against the half-baked dupes of ill-informed secularists who will assure him that the Gospels were written in the fourth century.

It would have made a considerable difference to me had I been told as a boy that whereas for all works of classical antiquity we have to depend on manuscripts written long after their original composition (350 years for Virgil, 500 for Horace, no less than 1,300 for Euripides), our great velum uncials of the New Testament were copied some 250 years after the date when the Gospels were first written. And since my boyhood, papyrus fragments of St. John have been found dating back to the beginning of the second century. All these facts, and many more, can be found in *The Story of the Bible*, by Sir Frederic Kenyon, for many years Keeper of the Manuscripts in the British Museum. *The Story of the Bible* is quite a small book, 130 pages of prewar economy printing, and perhaps even more suitable for use as a school textbook than those little books about Soviet Russia and Karl Marx that some enthusiasts are trying to force upon our secondary schools. Of course, it is very important that we should know more (a *great* deal more) about our Russian ally, but even if the Gospel of Christ were to vanish as completely from the world as the gospel of Karl Marx has, in effect, vanished from Russia, it would still be essential for those with any pretensions to culture to know something of the great religion that gave Europe her noblest architecture and art.

No such knowledge was regarded as essential in the school in which I was educated, and yet Edwardian Harrow certainly provided any boy who had an appetite for knowledge with the basis of a humanist culture, but one thing that was *not* taught at Harrow was the rational argument for the religion that was preached in the school chapel.

I entered Harrow in 1902. The Boer War, which had faintly disturbed the serene complacency of the Victorians, was drawing to a close. The dominant philosophy of the age was the belief in the perfectibility of man and the inevitability of progress. The Church of England appeared to be fighting a rearguard action against a confident secularism. Agnosticism was becoming fashionable. Lady Monkswell in the seventies recorded in her diary the horror of "Aunt Ena" at the thought that her sister-in-law should marry the infidel Leslie Stephen. "Mo says, 'How horrid; he is a brute.' But Lady Young says, 'He has such a tender heart, and he is obliged to turn a rough side to the world.'" The Hon. E.C.F. Collier, the editor of *A Victorian Diarist* (Mary, Lady Monkswell), adds, "The trouble here was that Mr. Leslie Stephen (later Sir Leslie Stephen) who had been in holy orders, had not only given them up, but had actually become an 'unbeliever.' The heinousness of this, in the eyes of that generation, can scarcely now be imagined. It placed one utterly beyond the pale."

But not for long. The Athenaeum is the favorite club of the Anglican hierarchy, and both Leslie Stephen, who popularized the word *agnostic*, and T. H. Huxley, who invented it, were elected to the Athenaeum under Rule 11; "distinguished Eminence in science, literature or the arts." Every headmaster from the foundation of Harrow in the Elizabethan age to the end of the first World War had been in holy orders. The last of this line of clerical head masters, the Rev. Lionel Ford, was a very devout Christian. It was even alleged that in his attitude to the staff, he allowed himself to be influenced by their interest in religion. I do not think that any such charge could have been substantiated against my own headmaster, the Rev. Joseph Wood, D.D.; one of the handsomest men I have ever met, a fine scholar, and a genial wit. It was his habit to invite the monitors in rotation to supper.

"I have just had a letter," he remarked to me when I supped with him, "from a parent who asks anxiously whether we have capital punishment at Harrow. I have replied, not as yet but when I introduce it, I shall begin with the masters." Now Dr. Wood would have urbanely agreed, had you remarked that spiritual health was more important than physical health, but though he would never have relaxed the rules, which forbade a boy to return to school if he was still in quarantine for an infectious disease, he would have been faintly amused had he been challenged to make some effort to inoculate Harrovians against the contagion of infidelity. He would, no doubt, have murmured polite assent, had you insisted that the disintegration of Christianity would produce results even more disastrous than those of the Black Death, but he would have firmly resisted any attempt to adapt the curriculum of a Christian school to the needs of a new age, in which Christianity was the subject of bitter and persistent attack.

The Harrow table of work (Classical side) for 1902 lies before me as I write. Excluding homework, we devoted about fifteen hours a week to the classics, and twelve to history, English, mathematics, and modern languages, and two hours to "Scripture." On Sunday afternoon, we yawned over the kings of Israel and Judah, and on Monday morning, we construed the Greek Testament. There was not the least reason why a conscientious agnostic should have hesitated to take the Scripture classes, for a man can teach Hebrew history and New Testament Greek without revealing his beliefs or disbeliefs, and those who did not believe were discreet. Once, it is true, after a boy had finished translating St. Luke's story of the earthquake that loosened the bonds of the prisoners, and thus freed Paul and Silas, the form master remarked sardonically, "In point of fact, it is not the function of earthquakes to facilitate the escape of convicts," but that was the only revealing comment I heard.

Apologetics—that is, the rational defense of Christianity—was not included among the subjects we studied at Harrow. My father was a Methodist, my mother a member of the Church of England, and I was brought up as an Anglican. I was prepared for confirmation by Sir Arthur Hort. Sir Arthur was the son of the Rev. Fenton Hort, a famous New Testament scholar and a founder of the Alpine Club.

And it was, of course, only in this latter capacity that I heard of him. Sir Arthur took me through the catechism, and made all the remarks that the occasion called for on the special temptations of youth, but said nothing that could be classified as apologetics. My brother was more fortunate. His tutor hinted at the existence of people who did not believe in God. "But of course," he said, "that's absurd. There's a reason for everything. We eat beef, and the cows eat grass, and God made the grass."

Sir Arthur Hort had not inherited his father's interest in New Testament criticism, but he was an enthusiastic Shakespearian. He encouraged me to enter for a Shakespeare prize, which I won, and as a result, I left Harrow aware of the reasons for supposing that the last act of *Henry VIII* was not written by Shakespeare, but unaware of the reasons for supposing that the Fourth Gospel was written by St. John. Of the many sermons I heard in the school chapel, one or two made an impression on me at the time, but I do not remember a single occasion on which a preacher gave us any reason to believe that Christianity was true.

Apologetics, not unnaturally, never intruded into the sermons we heard in the school chapel, all of which assumed the truth of Christianity, but it is only fair to add that the bishop who confirmed me mentioned the existence of unbelievers and provided us with yet another variant of the argument from design, a variant only slightly more persuasive than the man-cow-grass thesis with which my brother's tutor had endeavored to armor him against the arrows of unbelief. "At the universities, you will find men who openly deride the Christian faith. As I was coming up Harrow Hill today I heard a bird sing, and I felt more convinced than ever of the existence of a loving Father. Tell them *that*." I did not tell them that, perhaps, because the confirmation address had confirmed not my faith but my doubts. If that was the best that could be said for Christianity, it was time to see what could be said on the other side. I revered Leslie Stephens as the author of the most moving of all mountain books, *The Playground of Europe*, and I invested sixpence in a cheap reprint of his book, *An Agnostic's Apology*. The strong negations of the mountaineer soon drowned the twitterings of the bishop's bird.

My father could not help me, for he was not a rationalist. In defiance of his faith, he appealed not to reason but to personal experience. Prayer had enabled him to overcome temptation. I should have been impressed, if not converted, had he said to me, "The Resurrection is one of the most firmly established facts in history. Christianity can be proved to be true, and because Christianity is true, it is necessary to resist temptation in its most seductive form." Unattracted as I was by the consequences he invoked to justify his premise, and convinced that Christianity was irrational, I naturally declined to mortify my reason in order the more effectively to mortify my flesh.

I owe a great debt to my house master, the Rev. E.C.E. Owen, who lent me at this critical juncture two books that made an impression on me: William James's admirable lecture on *Immortality* and his *Will to Believe*. Agnostics may be divided into two classes: those who deny the possibility of religious knowledge and those who are content to assert that they have no such knowledge. *Ignoramus et ignorabimus* sums up the negations of the former; *ignoramus* of the latter.

Thanks to William James and to the difficulty of reconciling the quasi-mystical emotions evoked by mountain beauty with materialism, I had, at least, enough interest in religion to read the leading works, as they appeared, of the Modernists, such as Alfred Loisy, Alfred Leslie Lilley, the Liberal Jew C.G. Montefiore, Albert Schweizer, and George Tyrrell. Tyrrell had been educated at an Irish school of which my grandfather, Canon Moore, was the headmaster, and this fact sent me to his fascinating autobiography. I still think that his *Reflections on Catholicism*, written before his formal breach with Rome, is one of the most effective contributions to Catholic apologetics that I know. As editor of *The Isis*, the undergraduate paper, I coaxed review copies of these books out of the publishers, and a review of J.M. Thomson's *Jesus According to St. Mark* led to an acquaintance with the talented chaplain of Magdalen, whose book had just been enthusiastically welcomed by Anglican Modernists.

I accepted with uncritical faith the assumptions implicit in Modernist literature, first, that miracles are unthinkable and secondly, that Modernists welcome whereas traditionalists repudiate the assured results of modern scholarship. The first book that forced me to reexamine these assumptions was Bishop Lightfoot's rejoinder to *Supernatural Religion*. I was twenty-eight at the time. I was exploring Mr. Coolidge's library at Grindelwald when something prompted me to open Lightfoot's book. The author of *Supernatural Religion*, published in 1877, was a Modernist before the word *Modernism* was invented. He did his best to discredit miracles and to represent himself as a scholar of immense erudition. "This book," writes George Salmon, "obtained a good deal of notoriety by dint of enormous puffing, great pains having been taken to produce a belief that Bishop Thirlwall was the author. The aspect of the pages bristling with learned references, strengthened the impression that the author must be a man of immense reading. The windbag collapsed when Bishop Lightfoot showed that the supposed Bishop Thirlwall did not possess even a schoolboy acquaintance with Greek." In the same library, I found a copy of Dr. George Salmon's *A Historical Introduction to the Study of the Books of the New Testament*. Salmon was a brilliant mathematician and a Fellow of the Royal Society. He was also a brilliant New Testament scholar.

I have always been interested in the aesthetics of controversy, for controversy is one of the minor arts, and a well-built argument, like a well-built cathedral, is characterized by balance and proportion. I was delighted by the skill with which Lightfoot routed his opponent and the talent with which Salmon defended an indefensible case.

But was his case indefensible? By the time I had finished his book, I was beginning to have my doubts. My edition of Salmon, the seventh, is dated 1894, and the years that have passed since then have reinforced many of his arguments by the evidence of the papyrus fragments discovered in Egypt but have failed to produce any new fact to shake his conclusions. Salmon did not convince me, but he stimulated my curiosity and encouraged me to continue my researches. Among the many books that I read as the result of this initial impetus, I would like to single out for special mention those works of Sir William Ramsay quoted in the pages that follow, and *Who Moved the Stone?*, the author of which spent some years searching in vain for a natural explanation of the events of the first Easter Sunday.

The prejudices aroused in my mind by Modernist apologetics survived the discovery that the traditionalists had by far the better of the argument, and of these prejudices none resisted more stubbornly the pressure of fact than the favorite Modernist assumption that Modernists have the monopoly of exact and honest scholarship, and that Catholic contributions to New Testament criticism are vitiated by the need to conform to the decisions of the Church. As a result of this prejudice, I never read the contributions of Catholic scholars to the study of the Gospels until long after I had come to the conclusion that Christ rose from the dead. I have quoted sparingly in the pages that follow from Catholic writers, because my principal object in writing this book is to convert non-Christians to Christianity, and many of the readers who will, I hope, read this book will be the victim of prejudices very similar to mine, but it would be ungracious not to acknowledge my own debt to Catholic scholars such as Dom John Chapman, whose little book *The Four Gospels* is one of the best short introductions to the subject; the Rev. M.J. Lagrange, O.P.; the Rev. J.P. Arendzen, D.D.; and Père de Grandmaison, S.J. Of Père de Grandmaison's famous book *Jesus Christ*, an Anglican scholar, the Rev. H.P.V. Nunn, M.A., writes that he "cannot too highly commend this book to scholarly readers. It disproves completely the allegation that the Roman Catholic Modernists were brutally thrust out of the Church by mere authority. This book, and the similar works of M. Lepin and Fr. Lagrange, show that Modernism was fairly met in the French Church by courteous refutations and shown to be what it really is—nothing more nor less than a rehash of German theories with a dash of sentiment thrown in."

IV

"Nobody is ever converted by argument" is a popular slogan with Christian appeasers, but unilateral disarmament is as foolish in theological as in international disputes. Communists and atheists do not act on the principle that no Christian can ever be *perverted* by argument.

Nobody, of course, is ever *wholly* converted by argument, but if we exclude supernatural factors, argument is the decisive factor in many cases. It certainly was so in mine. I did not pray for guidance because I had abandoned, with relief, the practice of prayer while at Harrow. The empty tomb was a fascinating problem but—to me at that time—less interesting than those problems of snow and avalanche craft that I was trying to solve. My writings on snowcraft have emerged with credit from the test of scientific research, conducted in the main by Gerald Seligman, because I tried to practice what Huxley preached in the famous maxim "An assertion which outstrips the evidence is not only a blunder but a crime," and for the same reason, I was slow to commit myself to any definite theory about the Resurrection. The problems of snowcraft were scientific, the problem of the empty tomb historical, and in the latter case, as in the former, I tried to reach a solution by means of rational deductions from the available evidence. The mental process in both cases seemed to me much the same.

Whatever may be the influence of rational argument on conversion, it is certain that *lack* of rational argument is an important factor in perversion. Had I known what I now know, I would not, as a boy, have been perverted by the specious arguments of Leslie Stephen's *An Agnostic's Apology*. I have just reread a symposium, *Public School Religion*, which I edited and to which the Bishop of Bradford and the headmasters of Eton and Westminster contributed. Many of the points discussed would have been equally relevant in a wider setting than the public schools, as, for instance, the ingrained resistance of the average boy to anything that is taught as a school subject. But experience proves that where apologetics is intelligently taught, a surprisingly large number of boys are thereby inspired to propagate the Christian faith. In the final essay of this symposium, Christopher Hollis, at that time master at Stonyhurst, writes as follows:

> There is a class in apologetics. In such a class, just as in a class for trigonometry or for the reading of Catullus, there will be a few boys who are enthusiastically interested, a few to whom the subject is repugnant, the majority who accept the task to be done without fuss but also without enthusiasm. The proportions will vary with the liveliness of the master. Those boys who can take a delight in their work will rejoice, but the rest will not be such fools as to imagine that the primary question is whether their work—this particular work at any rate—"interests" them. They understand that they are taught apologetics not because they are interesting but because they are true. . . .
>
> *About two-thirds* of the upper boys belong to the voluntary Catholic Evidence Guild. The purpose of the Catholic Evidence Guild is to train speakers to defend the Catholic Faith in public speeches, and boys from the school do speak under its auspices both during the summer term at neighbouring towns and during the holidays. But, in order to qualify themselves to speak, they have first to join

a group, or class, presided over by a master, there to learn their subject and to pass a test in it.

I have taught apologetics at the great University of Notre Dame, Indiana, and I am unimpressed when people talk about the difficulty of interesting youth in the propagation of the Faith. One of my pupils, a born evangelist, made over twenty converts, most of them from materialism, within three years of leaving Notre Dame.

If apologetics is properly taught, even the idlest of pupils will at least discover that there is a rational case for religion, a case that can be defended with serene confidence against all opposition. There is a world of difference between leaving school ignorant of how to present the case for Christianity and leaving school ignorant that such a case exists.

The omission of apologetics, where apologetics is omitted, is defended on the ground that the curriculum is already overcrowded. It would be more honest to assert that Christianity does not matter than to suggest that it is not unreasonable that Christ should be crowded out of a Christian education. "*Because there was no room for him in the inn,*" but that particular innkeeper was not a humbug. He did not advertise that he made a special effort to cater for Christian clients.

I do not wish to belittle the difficulties. Schools that are in earnest about apologetics have to compete with those that are not. Apologetics is only a part, if the most important part, of religious instruction, but whatever else has to be cut down, the evidence for the central event in all human history should not be scamped.

"I think," writes Christopher Hollis, "that no Catholic teacher would deny that by far the most difficult part of his case [for Catholicism] is the demonstration of the divinity of Christ, and that once demonstrated, the rest of the apologetic is hardly more than formal. . . . I suppose there can hardly be any single person in England today, if there be one, who was brought up to believe in the Infallibility of the pope and who has subsequently rejected Infallibility but still retains the Incarnation. If there is, it would be interesting to know his name. That being so, it is but natural that the Catholic schoolmaster holds that the essential part of his apologetics is to persuade his pupils of the truth of the Incarnation, and that accomplished, the rest can almost be left to look after itself."

V

Modernism is merely a new name for a very old thing, Unitarianism, and Unitarianism is dynamic only when allied to a militant nationalism, as in the case of Mohammedanism. The Unitarianism of New England, for instance, is a mental climate rather than a religion. "Nothing quieted doubt so completely," wrote Henry Adams,

> as the mental calm of the Unitarian clergy. In uniform excellence of life and character, moral and

intellectual, the score of Unitarian clergymen about Boston, who controlled society and Harvard College were never excelled. They proclaimed as their merit that they insisted on no doctrine, but taught, or tried to teach the means of leading a virtuous, useful, unselfish life, which they held to be sufficient for salvation. For them difficulties might be ignored; doubts were waste of thought; nothing exacted solution. Boston had solved the universe; or had offered and realised the best solution yet tried. The problem was worked out.

Of all the conditions of his youth which afterwards puzzled the grown-up man, the disappearance of religion puzzled him most. The boy went to church twice every Sunday; he was taught to read his Bible, and he learned religious poetry by heart; he believed in a mild deism; he prayed; he went through all the forms; but neither to him nor his brothers or sisters was religion real. Even the mild discipline of the Unitarian Church was so irksome that they all threw it off at the first possible moment, and never afterwards entered a church. The religious instinct had vanished, and could not be revived, although one made in later life many efforts to recover it.

The honest Unitarian who describes himself as such is no danger to Christianity so long as he attacks the Church from without, but the camouflaged Unitarian is the most effective of all allies of the Antichrist. In Latin countries, people who repudiate the deity of our Lord do not describe themselves as Christians and are consequently far less dangerous than those who rob the word *Christian* of all meaning by annexing it for an anti-Christian theology. In the Latin south, the enemies of Christianity often make their position clear by burning a church. In England, we don't burn churches; we empty them. We solve our problems by ignoring them and are more loyal to names than to principles, with the result that many a man who repudiates the basic dogmas of Christianity would be most incensed if you denied his right to the Christian name.

Let me quote in this connection an unsigned article in the *Church Times* (December 15, 1944) entitled "Trinitarians or Unitarians." The article, which was an attempt to discover what "nominal Christians" believe, was based on several thousand questions asked about religion by members of the Services: "Time and again I have met men and women who regard themselves as nominal members of a Christian denomination either Anglican or Nonconformist, and yet have denied that Jesus Christ was the son of God. . . . Few such critics show any sign of knowing that their heretical views place them outside the tenets of the faith they claim to hold." And he points out that the churches which claim thousands of nominal members in the Services "ignore the fact that many of their adherents repudiate categorically essential doctrines. *They are self-styled Trinitarians with Unitarian convictions. Here is one of the fundamental reasons why the churches remain empty* —why this huge army of young people never show any desire to enter the House of God" (italics mine).

The Anglican who wrote this article would have had no grievance against an honest Unitarian who described himself as such, but he is justly angered by those disciples of Humpty Dumpty who misuse the great word *Christian*. "'When I use a word,' Humpty Dumpty said in a scornful tone, 'it means just what I choose it to mean, neither more nor less.'" And there are many people who seem to think that they can make the word *Christian* mean "a man who reveres in Jesus a liberal-minded progressive, who taught that there is a lot to be said for loving one's neighbor, and who went about healing people who had nothing much the matter with them."

The trouble with Unitarianism is that it has no standing. It has neither cathedrals nor endowments, neither historical traditions nor social prestige. But though Unitarians have no hope of competing successfully against the national church, they need not despair of annexing it. Their "Trojan Horse technique" has succeeded all too well in Continental Protestantism, where the prestige of the Christian name and the associations of the Christian centuries have been successfully exploited to promote a rival firm.

When the Catholic Church excommunicated the Unitarians who described themselves as Modernists, she was denounced not only for her intolerance but for her folly in driving such eminent scholars as Loisy into the wilderness. It is, of course, no more "intolerant" of a church to excommunicate those who repudiate her basic doctrines than for a political party to exclude those who repudiate the party platform. Nobody would accuse Dr. Inge of ultraconservative tendencies in doctrine. He is a Modernist, but a Modernist with a difference, for his theology is Christocentric. After summarizing the views of Loisy and other Modernists, he adds, "What more, it may well be asked, have rationalist opponents of Christianity ever said, in their efforts to tear up the Christian religion by the roots, than we find here admitted by Catholic apologists? What is left of the object of the Church's worship if the Christ of history was but an enthusiastic Jewish peasant whose pathetic ignorance of the forces opposed to Him led Him to the absurd enterprise of attempting a *coup d'etat* at Jerusalem?"

"L'historien," writes Loisy, "n'a pas à s'inspirer de l'agnosticisme pour écarter Dieu de l'histoire; il ne l'y rencontre jamais." "It would be more accurate," Dr. Inge remarks, "to say that, whenever the meeting takes place 'the historian' gives the other the cut direct."

During fifty years of religious decline, the only religious communion in the United Kingdom that has increased its regular communicants is the Catholic Church, and it is no coincidence that the Catholic Church is the one church that is completely immune from the Unitarian microbe.

If further evidence is needed of the destructive influence of this infection, all that is necessary is to contrast the comparative strength of Anglicanism, which is still predominantly Trinitarian, with the moribund condition of Continental Protestantism.

My father convened many Reunion Conferences at Grindelwald and Murren, and among those who attended were representatives of German, Swiss, and French Protestants. I have met hundreds of Swiss, German, and French skiers and mountaineers who would enter themselves on a census form as Lutherans or Calvinists or Zwinglians but, as it happens, I have never met a young skier or mountaineer who is a regular attendant at any Protestant place of worship. The Continental pastors, whom I met at Murren and elsewhere, reminded me of the battalions that Kerensky tried to form when the Russian army was disintegrating, battalions composed solely of officers.

The same tendencies that sterilized Continental Protestantism may be observed in Anglicanism, and efforts are being made to endow Unitarianism at the expense of the taxpayer in a country in which Christianity is the established religion.

In *The Christian* of September 23, 1943, a letter appeared that was signed "G. Wilson."

> I have just returned [wrote Mr. Wilson] from a special Divinity course for schoolteachers and others at Oxford University and beg to be allowed to draw the

attention of your readers to the true nature of this course, which is recognised by the Board of Education as the means of further qualifying teachers to take their part in the new "Religion in Schools" campaign. The course was openly used as a means of propagating the doctrines of "Higher Criticism" and by the end of the week the orthodox Christian faith was denuded of its fundamentals. We were informed that modern scholarship had entirely altered traditional Christianity. There was no Virgin Birth. The Resurrection of Christ and the Appearances were only "spiritual" not physical, and the question of the empty tomb could be explained by the fact that the women and the disciples probably returned to the wrong tomb, but in any case, the body would disintegrate very quickly in such a climate and little trace would be left in three days! [And this is the kind of rubbish solemnly taught by people who invent an imaginary conflict between Christianity and science in order to engineer a bogus reconciliation.]

There were about eighty teachers from all parts of the country attending the course and a great many appeared to accept this travesty of Christian belief without question. If, therefore, these unsound doctrines are soon to be propagated throughout the schools of the country, one wonders whether it would not be better to advocate the abolition of the Scripture lesson entirely.

Three headmasters who attended the course signed a declaration that the statements in this letter were correct.

One need not be an Anglican to realize what this country would lose if Anglicanism were destroyed from within by the Trojan horse of Unitarianism.

Fortunately, the Church of England, like England, has unsuspected powers of recuperation. Her position in the middle of the eighteenth century seemed desperate. "It has come I know not how," wrote the eighteenth-century Bishop Butler, "to be taken for granted by many persons that Christianity is not so much a subject of inquiry; but that it is, now at length, discovered to be fictitious. And accordingly they treat it as if, in the present age, this were an agreed point among all persons of discernment; and nothing remained but to set it up as a principal subject of mirth and ridicule, as it were by reprisals, for its having so long interrupted the pleasures of the world."

A few years later, John Wesley, the greatest Englishman of the eighteenth century, laid the foundations of the Methodism that re-Christianized multitudes who had drifted away from the national church.

Deism was an even greater danger to the Church of England in the eighteenth century than Modernism in the twentieth. "The Church as it now is," wrote Dr. Arnold in the early years of the nineteenth century, "no human power can save." Within a few years, the Oxford Movement had revolutionized the situation and refuted the pessimists.

When I was a boy, Anglican and Nonconformist churches were fuller than they are today, and there was far less open repudiation of Christian doctrine and morals among those who never attended a place of worship, but I do not think that the number of genuinely convinced Christians was much larger. It was still the fashion to go to church, but many of those who did were secretly convinced that science had disproved miracles.

Today the old bogey, the alleged conflict between science and religion, survives only in the writings of people like Mr. Harold Laski, who are out of touch with modern thought. A popular modern line is to insist that miracles are so common that they prove nothing. When I was a boy, many Christians were infected by defeatism and doubt, and materialism appeared triumphant. Today it is the materialists, the Dawnists, and the Utopians who are fighting a desperate rearguard action, and as a result many who have rejected Christianity are prepared to reexamine the case for religion. The substitutes for Christianity have failed. Hedonism has not made men happy. Utopianism has not brought Utopia any nearer. Humanitarianism has not made men humane, and high-minded secularism has not made them good.

Herein lies our opportunity, an opportunity that is a test of courage. Nothing is to be gained by appeasement. Those who are anxious to adapt their beliefs to every changing fad and fashion of political and pseudoscientific thought make no converts. The Church has, of course, not

only the right but the duty to proclaim the social consequences of Christianity and to denounce social injustice,
but overemphasis on the secular implications of Christianity is always (and rightly) interpreted as lack of confidence
in the supernatural foundation.

First things must come first. *The British Weekly* describes itself as a "journal of social and religious progress"
that reverses the proper order of priority, for social progress is the *consequence* of the progress that consists in the
approach to God, and there can be no social progress in
an age of religious regress.

The Church is not competing with secular politicians
for our support. Christ does not ask for our support. He
demands our obedience. Christians have been far too
defensive, and I agree with an Anglican, Prebendary E.
Moore Darling, who wrote to me as follows. "May I add
that we do too much defense. Our work should begin
with a full-blooded attack: 'The appalling difficulties of
unbelief.'"

Courage is the basic virtue, and the man with the
courage of his convictions will always command respect
and sometimes assent—even when he asks for sacrifices
instead of offering bribes. Of the few, the tragically few,
speeches by democratic politicians that are immortal, the
greatest was that in which a prime minister of England
offered his countrymen not security, nor a higher standard
of living, but "blood, sweat, and tears." To such an appeal
the best in man will always respond.

XLVI

On a tort de parler des consolations de la religion, dit Ensénat. On doit dire: les terribles vérités chrétiennes.[1] An exaggeration, for it is right to speak of the consolations of religion but wrong to ignore the "terrible Christian truths." And of these truths, none is more terrible than the fact that the individual or the country that rejects what God proposes for our belief must inevitably perish.

In his remarkable book *The Religious Prospect*, Canon V. A. Demant writes: "The Christian religion is primarily a religion of redemption, a gospel. It is good news, not a philosophy, or good advice." The first question we ask about news is whether it is reliable, and the most important thing about Christianity is that it is *true*. "If Christ has not been raised, then our proclamation has been in vain and your faith has been in vain" (1 Cor. 15:14). A generation that has tasted the bitter fruits of a false philosophy is readier than its grandfathers to reexamine the great question. Did Christ rise from the dead? It is the truth of Christianity, rather than its social consequences, that excites increasing interest.

I recently spent half an hour examining the books displayed on a railway bookstall in a big industrial town. Mr. C.S. Lewis's books were prominently displayed. The popularity of his admirable works of Christian apologetics is clear evidence of an increasing demand for undiluted

---

[1] "It is wrong to speak of religion's consolations, said Ensénat. We must say. terrible Christian truths."

Christianity. The bookstall also catered to all those who were anxious to be well informed about Soviet Russia. There were no books by our Christian appeasers.

In my experience, people who attack the Church for the alleged alliance with the rich are not looking for the truth. They are looking for a scrap. The genuine inquirer knows that the Church is a mixed bag, not an exclusive club from which Tories are blackballed and to which only Progressives are admitted. The genuine inquirer is not much interested in the politics of ecclesiastics and is as unlikely to take his own politics from a primate as his religion from a prime minister. He is in search of something very different, of the answer to the ultimate problems. Does God exist? Is life nothing but a futile flicker of uneasy consciousness between the darkness of the womb and the darkness of the tomb? Did Christ rise from the dead? It is the bankruptcy of Utopianism that is forcing so many people to reconsider the Christian claims. The churches that are full are those in which men are promised not Utopia on earth, but those in which they are reminded that the inescapable sufferings of this life are as nothing compared with the happiness that God has prepared for those who love him.

VI

And now all that remains is to record my gratitude to those who have helped me, to Father T.J. Crompton, S.J., a great expert on the New Testament, for his kindly verdict on the manuscript, submitted to him by the publishers, and for some very helpful suggestions, and to Lt. Col. B. W. Bowdler, C.M.G., D.S.O., who has read the proofs of this book and found them, I hope, a pleasant change from the proofs of the *British Ski Year Book*, which owe so much to his careful reading.

Believing, as I do, that footnotes should be reduced to a minimum, I have relegated to the end of the book references, translations of such passages as are not included in the text, including a translation of the dedicatory poem, and also notes. Points of secondary interest are relegated to the notes, as are also some popular "difficulties," such as the alleged resemblance between Christianity and Buddhism.

If I were in danger of doubting the increasing interest in religion, my postbag would soon convince me. I have had no secretary since the war, but I have answered every letter I have received, with the exception of those from lunatics, those which are purely abusive, and those that I have lost. I am not the tidiest of men, and letters have a way of drifting off the edge of my table into the wastepaper basket. My conscience is tortured by the memory of letters mislaid before I could reply to them, and I am therefore more than grateful to kind people who send stamped and addressed envelopes, for I seldom lose *both* the letter and the envelope enclosed for the reply.

Arnold Lunn
Christmas Day 1944

ONE

The Scientific Approach
to the Miraculous

S IR WILLIAM RAMSAY WAS a convinced anti-miraculist
when he began his great career as an archaeologist
in Asia Minor, but his mind, unlike those of most anti-
miraculists, was not closed to evidence that conflicted with
his prejudices. In the opening chapter of his book *Luke the
Physician*, which embodied the results of thirty-four years
of research, he writes as follows. "The question 'Shall we
hear evidence or not?' presents itself at the threshold of
every investigation into the New Testament. Modern criticism for a time entered on its task with a decided negative.
Its mind was made up, and it would not listen to evidence
on a matter that was already decided."

To the question "Shall we hear evidence or not?" David
Friedrich Strauss, Émile Zola, and the Modernists reply

with an unhesitating negative, so far at least as the evidence for miracles is concerned.

"Wherever anything occurs," Ramsay continues, "that savours of the marvellous in the estimation of the polished and courteous scholar, sitting in his well-ordered library and contemplating the world through its windows, it must be forthwith set aside as unworthy of attention and as mere delusion. *That method of studying the first century was the method of the later nineteenth century. I venture to think that it will not be the method of the twentieth century.* If you have ever lived in Asia you know that a great religion does not establish itself without some unusual accompaniments. The marvellous result is not achieved without some marvellous preliminaries." The sentence that I have italicized contains a prediction that I believe to be in the process of verification. The attitude of the twentieth century to supernatural and supernormal phenomena differs even now, and will probably differ to an even greater degree, from the attitude of the nineteenth century.

The *alleged* cause of the anti-miraculist attitude of the nineteenth century was the progress of science. Christians and anti-Christians were keenly interested in the alleged conflict between science and religion. The truth is that every advance of science has reinforced, if only indirectly, the case for miracles. It is, for instance, because our knowledge of medical science is increasing that we can assert with increasing confidence that certain cures at Lourdes are inexplicable within the framework of natural causes.

The greater our knowledge of natural agencies, the greater our ability to isolate and recognize the effects produced by supernatural agencies.

Man, animals, vegetables, and the inanimate forces of nature, such as sun, frost, and running water, are natural agencies. Is the world in which we live, and are the terrestrial phenomena that we observe, *solely* due to natural agencies? Or are there some phenomena that are due to supernatural agencies?

The determination to exclude miracles from the field of research, which Ramsay maintains to have been characteristic of the nineteenth century, was in no way the result of a devotion to science. On the contrary, it was, as we shall see, a recrudescence in a modern form of certain tendencies that effectively hampered the advance of science in the Middle Ages.

The Church, except in the case of Galileo, never came into conflict with scientists on a scientific issue. It was the petrifying influence of Aristotle that obstructed research. Aristotle himself was a great naturalist, but though the observation of nature in general and of the animal kingdom in particular was the basis of his conclusions, those conclusions had constantly to be readjusted to suit the requirements of certain dogmas that Aristotle made no attempt either to prove by reason or to check by observation.

Thus, the Aristotelian system of physics had to accommodate itself to the following dogmas. All matter is made up of four elements: earth, air, fire, and water. The earth is the center of the universe. Circular movement is the most perfect conceivable, and *therefore* the stars and planets move in concentric circles around the earth.

That it was not the influence of the Church but the influence of a mode of thinking that can be traced back to Aristotle which impeded the advance of science can be proved, among other things, by the type of error that is so common in the writings of that great Protestant Lord Bacon. For example, he gravely assures us that wooden arrows without an iron point penetrate farther into wooden substance than the same arrows pointed with iron, owing to "similitude of substance." And it was not the fear of ecclesiastical censure that prevented Caesar Cremonini from looking through Galileo's telescope but the fear of finding Aristotle's physics were wrong. Again and again the pioneers of astronomy in Europe, as Mr. Hinks points out in his book *Astronomy* (Home University Library), were met "with the objection that Aristotle said so and so. Now what Aristotle said was founded upon the vaguest kind of information. Planets must move in circles because the circle is the only 'perfect' figure. Seven is a perfect number, and therefore if you have found seven of a thing you need not waste time looking for an eighth."

The alleged perfection of the circle and of the figure seven conform not to a scientific but to an *aesthetic* criterion, and aesthetic criteria play a much greater part in the shaping of scientific hypotheses than scientists would be prepared to admit.

Kepler's career bridges the medieval and the modern attitude to science. He was, at first, greatly influenced by aesthetic criteria. At that time, only six planets had been discovered, and Kepler was immensely elated when he discovered that "five regular solids" could be inserted between the spheres of the six planets. He believed that this fact, which, even if it were true, we should regard as absolutely irrelevant, was a sufficient explanation of the planets' being six in number. And because the circle was more "perfect" than the ellipse, he made eighteen successive attempts to adapt the planetary movements to a circular orbit before he finally adopted ellipses. In the end, observation triumphed over aesthetic prejudices.

Why was the circle considered more perfect than the ellipse? Probably because it was simpler. Simplicity has not only an aesthetic attraction but an obvious appeal to all those oppressed by the complexity of phenomena. It is always tempting to search for a shortcut to a solution by eliminating as many unknown factors as possible. "It is impossible," as Mr. A. G. Tansley remarks, "to overemphasize the overmastering desire of the human mind for some kind of unification—for having a single consistent or seemingly consistent scheme which appears to include and reconcile contradictory things." It is, indeed, a natural and human weakness to hope that all difficulties of life will yield to some simple panacea. In politics, we are invited to abandon the complexity of the democratic solution reasonably fair to all classes, in favor of the dictatorship of one particular class, the proletariat. In biology, Darwin tries to explain evolution by the sole agency of natural selection. The materialist explains all phenomena in terms of matter, the Christian Scientist in terms of mind, the Freudian in terms of sex.

It is this desire to simplify a complex problem, this urge toward unification that explains the prejudice of the anti-miraculist, for if all phenomena could be explained solely in terms of natural agencies, the task of the scientists would be simplified. The aesthetic criterion invoked in one age to prove that planets must move in circles is invoked a few centuries later to prove that miracles do not occur, for miracles are untidy and unpredictable intrusions into a neat and orderly universe, ugly discords in the beautiful uniformity of nature. The medieval outlook effectively prevented astronomical discovery. The neo-medievalism of the anti-miraculist sterilizes research in a field of inquiry infinitely more important than that in which Galileo and Kepler achieved fame.

Are terrestrial phenomena influenced by supernatural agencies? Is there any evidence for life beyond the grave? Questions such as these are *infinitely* more important than those with which Kepler was concerned, but the conventional scientists of the nineteenth century, when invited to investigate supernormal phenomena, refused to admit that the reality of supernatural or supernormal agencies was a proper subject for scientific research. Huxley, for instance, when invited to examine the curious phenomena produced by the medium Home, reacted precisely as did

6

Cremonini when asked to look through Galileo's telescope at the moons of Jupiter, whose existence conflicted with Aristotle's physics.

The anti-miraculist fashion might have been less influential but for the fact that it was in accord with political fashion. *Deism*, the belief that God may have created the universe but never interferes in the processes of creation, originated in England at the time of the "Glorious Revolution," which substituted a limited for an absolute monarch. The King of England has a theoretical right to veto laws that have been approved by Parliament. The God of deism has a theoretical right to veto the laws of nature, but neither the King of England nor the King of Kings would be so unconstitutional as to exercise these rights. Deism might be defined as constitutional theism. Miracles are as objectionable to the deist as the arbitrary acts of a constitutional monarch are to the Liberal. In the sphere of economics, constitutional theism found expression in the doctrines of *laissez-faire* Liberalism. God might reign, but he could not rule. Malthus, a kindly Anglican clergyman, explained that if children were born in excess of the requirements of the labor market, then both parents and children should be left to starve. Even God, it seemed, could not veto the laws of political economy.

II

There is no sounder approach to the problem of miracles than the method that led to the discovery of the planet

Neptune. The orbit of a planet is determined by the interplay of the major attraction exerted by the sun and the lesser pulls of the other planets. In spite of the complexity of the problem, the course of a planet can be accurately predicted. Now, before the discovery of the planet Neptune, astronomers were bewildered by certain "perturbations" in the planetary orbits, that is, by their deviations from the orbits as predicted. Le Verrière subjected these "perturbations" to a searching analysis and came to the conclusion that they could not be explained in terms of known agencies, that is, as the consequence of the forces exerted by the sun and by the planets known, at that time, to exist. He therefore assumed that the perturbations must have been due to the action of an unknown agency, an undiscovered planet. As a result of his calculations, the planet Neptune was located on September 23, 1846, within a degree of the point where Le Verrière had announced that the undiscovered planet would be found.

Note that Le Verrière's discovery began by the proof of a purely negative conclusion, the conclusion that the orbits of the planets could not be wholly explained in terms of known agencies. The method of Le Verrière can be employed to solve a problem of infinitely greater importance than the problem of planetary perturbations.

The Oxford Dictionary defines a miracle as a "marvelous event due to some supernatural agency." Let us define a miracle, provisionally, as a "perturbation inexplicable in terms of natural agencies."

The true scientist will start his investigation unhampered by negative dogmas. He will not assume the nonexistence of supernatural agencies, but he will make every effort to explain terrestrial phenomena in terms of natural agencies. Like Le Verrière, he will attempt to exhaust the possibility that a given phenomenon has been caused by known agencies before considering the possibility that it has been caused by an unknown agency.

The scientific approach to this problem is less uncommon in scientific circles than was the case in the nineteenth century, but the man in the street is still influenced by the negative dogmatism of the old-fashioned secularist who repeated with simple faith Matthew Arnold's remark: "Miracles don't occur."

The nineteenth-century secularist did not test his conclusions by the evidence; he tested the evidence by its conformity to his beliefs. Thus Strauss, author of the notorious *Life of Jesus*, laid down as a canon of New Testament criticism the principle, "In the person and acts of Jesus there was nothing supernatural," and he accordingly dates the Gospels on the assumption that miracles must be a later interpolation. Zola, like Strauss, accepted with simple faith the unproved and unprovable dogma that the natural world is a closed system and that supernatural agencies do not exist. Zola's negative faith was proof against the stubborn fact of the two miracles that he himself witnessed at Lourdes, of which the first was the sudden cure of an advanced stage of lupus. Zola describes Marie Lemarchand's condition as he saw her on the way to Lourdes. "It was," writes Zola, "a case of lupus which had preyed upon the unhappy woman's nose and mouth. Ulceration had spread and was hourly spreading and devouring the membrane in its progress. The cartilage of the nose was almost eaten away, the mouth was drawn all on one side by the swollen condition of the upper lip. The whole was a frightful distorted mass of matter and oozing blood." Zola's account is incomplete, for the patient was coughing and spitting blood. The apexes of both lungs were affected, and she had sores on her leg. Dr. d'Hombres saw her immediately before and immediately after she entered the bath. "Both her cheeks, the lower part of her nose, and her upper lip were covered with a tuberculous ulcer and secreted matter abundantly. On her return from the baths I at once followed her to the hospital. I recognised her quite well although her face was entirely changed. Instead of the horrible sore I had so lately seen, the surface was red, it is true, but dry and covered with a new skin. The other sores had also dried up in the piscina." The doctors who examined her could find nothing the matter with the lungs and testified to the presence of the new skin on her face.

Zola was there. He had said, "I only want to see a cut finger dipped in water and come out healed." "Behold the case of your dreams, M. Zola," said the president of the medical bureau, presenting the girl whose hideous disease had made such an impression on the novelist before the cure. "Ah no!" said Zola, "I do not want to look at her.

She is still too ugly," alluding to the red color of the new skin. Before he left Lourdes, Zola recited his credo to the president: "Were I to see all the sick at Lourdes cured, I would not believe in a miracle."

The modern skeptic is less dogmatic than Zola. Many such skeptics would admit the fact that inexplicable cures take place at Lourdes but refuse to believe that they are due to supernatural agencies. Thus Professor J.B.S. Haldane, F.R.S., the distinguished biologist, who exchanged letters with me that were published under the title *Science and the Supernatural*, and who attacked not only Christianity but theism in the course of our correspondence, wrote as follows: "Still, one or two of the more surprising Lourdes miracles, such as the immediate healing of a suppurating fracture of eight years' standing, seem to me to be possibly true, and, if so, very remarkable and worth investigating, although if they were shown to be true they would not prove the particular theory of their origin current at Lourdes" (p. 13). Haldane contends that sooner or later, science will explain such alleged miracles in terms of natural law.

Now the question we are seeking to solve is whether supernatural agencies exist. This is the subject of our research. Clearly we may as well abandon the research if all evidence that suggests supernatural agencies is to be explained away as the result of our ignorance. There must be something wrong with a method that starts by assuming the nonexistence of an agent whose existence or nonexistence is the occasion of our research. This is merely Strauss's formula in a modern dress. "In the phenomena of this terrestrial planet, no supernaturalism shall be allowed to remain."

Had Le Verrière adopted this method, he would never have discovered Neptune. It is our ignorance, he would have argued, that is responsible for the attribution of these perturbations to an unknown planet. Sooner or later science will resolve the apparent discrepancies and prove that these tiresome perturbations are wholly consistent with our belief that the planetary system, as we know it, is a closed system subject to no external influences.

Clearly, if the Haldane criterion is accepted, all further investigation is futile. Even if supernatural agencies exist, we are absolved from recognizing their existence, for we can always appeal to the science of the future to explain the perturbations in terms of the agencies we already know. According to pious legend, St. Denis is alleged to have carried his head in his hands after he had been decapitated. Had Haldane met St. Denis, he would perhaps have remarked "very remarkable and worth investigating, but science will one day explain the fact that certain unusual pathological types can survive decapitation for an appreciable time." Similarly Le Verrière, had he accepted the obligation to explain all planetary perturbations in terms of the planets that were known to him, might have appealed to the science of the future to explain the unaccountable deviations of planets from their predicted courses without prejudice to the accepted hypothesis that the planets then known constituted a closed system. But there must be something wrong with a method of research that effectively debars the investigator from discovering an unknown agent, the nature and reality of which is the subject of research.

"How can the assumption," writes Mr. Malcolm Grant, "of unknown laws or of unknown natural causes be better *science* than the determination to abide by recognised, fundamental, so-to-say necessary and obvious laws, to abide by careful observation and by enlightened failure?" "Enlightened" because the failure to discover natural agents throws light on the existence of supernatural agents.

Mr. Grant would not accept the Catholic explanation of the Lourdes miracles, but the quotation that I have taken from his book *A New Argument for God and Survival* (Faber and Faber) continues: "The 'rationalist' who denies the reality of, for instance, all well-attested cures at Lourdes (cures of organic diseases) is a fool; but what shall we call the man who assumes, and keeps on assuming even after careful study, that they are natural events?"

Finally, there are those who contend that God is not included in the scientist's terms of reference, and that the scientist cannot reasonably be asked to express a scientific opinion on the miracles at Lourdes, or elsewhere. His task is to interpret phenomena in terms of natural agents and natural law.

The word *science* is derived from *scientia*, which means "knowledge." A correct explanation of a given phenomenon that enlightens us as to its cause is *scientific*, whether that cause is a natural or a supernatural agent. There is not the least scientific justification for the belief that a particular group of agents must be excluded from the field of research. This is as if Le Verrière had been restricted by his terms of reference to explaining all planetary "perturbations" in terms of planetary agents known to, and classified by, astronomers.

The scientist is not asked for a *positive* verdict in support of the existence of supernatural agencies. His more modest role is to answer the question: "Can this phenomenon be explained in terms of natural agencies?" All that we demand from the scientist is an answer to a question that is within his competence to decide.

There are no doubt some survivors of the Victorian rationalists who continue to assert that science has disproved the possibility of miracles. This happens to be the exact reverse of the truth. It is only because we believe in science that we believe in miracles. It is only because we have faith in the account that the scientist gives of natural phenomena that we dare to assert that a particular phenomenon was not caused by natural agents. "What makes it difficult for us to believe in miracles," writes Msgr. Ronald Knox, "is not human science; it is human nescience." It is because our knowledge of the laws of nature is limited that in case after case which looks like a miracle we cannot be quite certain that those laws have been modified or suspended by a supernatural power. Even of the best-attested Lourdes miracles we do not say that a "miracle is theologically certain; we only say that it is, so far, the best account we can give of the facts. We differ from our critics only in this," Msgr. Knox continues, "that we say, 'It may be a miracle or it may not,' whereas they say, 'Whatever it is, it certainly is not a miracle.' Which side approaches the subject with an open mind, and in a spirit of enquiry? Which side approaches the subject encumbered with the burden of dogmatic prepossession? Which side faces the facts?"

Finally, there is the so-called historical argument. "The historical argument," writes Haldane, "appeals to me. In primitive societies, such as those of West and Central Africa, all phenomena not understood, e.g., all non-violent deaths, are put down to the activity of spirits. As knowledge increases, more and more of them are explained in other ways. There are now rather few left over in which the intervention of spirits is in the least plausible."

If phenomena may be divided into two classes, those that are directly caused by a supernatural agent, and those that are caused by a natural agent, the mistake of incorrect classification is admittedly more likely to be made by a primitive savage than by a modern scientist and the transference of some phenomena from the supernatural to the natural class is a probable result of the advance of science. And yet this sequence of events, *which is inevitable if miracles occur*, is cited by Haldane as an argument against the occurrence of miracles. "If A is true, then B must happen," is our case. "But B happens, therefore A is untrue," replies Haldane. His argument is neither historical nor logical.

People who appeal to the so-called "historical argument" often fail to distinguish between the reactions of primitive savages and medieval men to the miraculous. All those who were born before the scientific age are assumed to have been equally credulous and to have lived in a constant expectation of miracles. This is very far from being the case. Miracles occurred in the Middle Ages as they occur today, but the overwhelming majority of Christians then as now, lived and died without witnessing a phenomenon that they believed to be miraculous. History is, in the main, the record of the exceptional, and consequently we are tempted to assume that miracles were more common in past ages than in our own, a common illusion among the pious. St. Gregory, for instance, writing within six centuries of the Crucifixion, raises this same complaint, and looks back with much the same regret to the Apostolic Age.

"Ah, but if a medieval man," retorts the skeptic, "had been transported forward through the centuries, he would have attributed the voice of the BBC announcer emerging from a portable wireless to some supernatural agency." Would he? Some would, and others wouldn't. The proportion of the credulous to the critical was no greater in the thirteenth than in the twentieth century. Professor F.M. Powicke, the eminent medievalist, endorses and makes his own the remark that "never in the whole history of the world did so many people believe so firmly in so many things, the authority for which they could not test, as do Londoners today." And in any case what concerns us is not the cause of error in classification that leads the uncritical to classify natural events as miracles, or the proportion of people in every age who fall into this error, but whether, in point of fact, there is a basic distinction between those marvels of modern science which we owe to the ingenuity of man, and those miracles, such as the miracles of healing at Lourdes, which the ingenuity of man can neither duplicate nor explain.

Haldane's assumption that there has been a continuous transference of phenomena from the allegedly supernatural to the admittedly natural class is unhistorical. Every century contributes its quota to the class of phenomena that resists all attempts at explanation in terms of natural agents. Furthermore, the process of transferring doubtful cases from one class to another is not a one-way process. In the late nineteenth century, it was the fashion in scientific circles to write as if, eventually, all phenomena that had once been classified as supernatural would, in the course of time, be explained by science within the framework of her accepted categories, but there are few scientists today who would assert that all supernormal phenomena can be explained as the result of fraud, hallucination, or inaccurate observation. It is materialism, not supernaturalism, which is fighting today a desperate rearguard action against enlightened science.

TWO

Modern Miracles

G OD NORMALLY WORKS THROUGH secondary causes. The seed is sown, the wheat shoots up and matures, and the baker converts the wheat into bread. But in rare and exceptional instances God suspends for a moment the operation of those laws of nature that owe their existence and validity to him alone, and expresses his will more directly, and performs without the aid of secondary causes what he is continually doing by means of secondary causes. "Just in the millionth instance he multiplies bread instead of multiplying the wheat" and feeds the five thousand without the intervention of secondary causes.

A miracle is not the violation of a law of nature. An apple falls from the branch of a tree toward the grass immediately below. Science insists that this apple will inevitably reach the ground *unless an agent arrests its passage through the air*. I put out my hand and catch the apple. No law of nature is violated. The law of gravitation, for instance, continues to operate, and produces on my outstretched hand the sensation of weight, as the hand checks the downward flight of the apple. All that has happened is that my *human* will has modified some of the effects that normally follow when an apple falls to the ground.

A miracle might be defined as the modification of the normal course of nature by divine will. That there is no *a priori* objection to miracles is conceded by the eminent agnostic John Stuart Mill. "The interference," he writes, "of human will with the course of Nature is not an exception to law: and by the same rule interference by the divine will would not be an exception, either."

A miracle is a form of divine creative activity. "The *a priori* arguments against theism, and, given a deity, against the possibility of creative acts," wrote T.H. Huxley, "appear to me devoid of reasonable foundation."

If, then, there is a God, neither science nor philosophy forbids us to believe in the *possibility* of miracles. We must not, of course, equate the *absence* of *a priori* arguments against the existence of God or against the possibility of miracles with the evidence we require to prove that God exists and that miracles occur, but at least we can begin our research unhampered by the negative dogmas of old-fashioned secularists. The question as to whether miracles are possible has been decided in the affirmative. The question as to whether miracles happen can be decided, and can be decided only, by examining the evidence for alleged miracles in accordance with the exacting standards of historical and scientific research.

I propose to devote this chapter to an examination of the better-attested modern miracles, that is, the miracles at Lourdes. It is possible to admit that cures, inexplicable by science, have been observed at Lourdes and yet to deny the existence of God. This would seem to be the position adopted by Professor J.B.S. Haldane, F.R.S. Again, it is possible to accept these miracles as evidence of the interference by divine will with the course of nature and yet refuse to accept the Catholic interpretation of these miracles, and it is, of course, also possible for old-fashioned obscurantists to leave unexamined the evidence for these miracles on the ground that it is impossible to reconcile the reality of miracles with the dogmas of their reactionary sects.

The alleged miracles of Lourdes have a special claim to scientific consideration for two reasons. First, because the cures are examined by a specially constituted committee of doctors. Christian Scientists are notoriously unfriendly to medical scrutiny, but doctors, irrespective of religion or nationality, are invited to serve on the medical Bureau des Constatations, which was established in 1882 to test the alleged miraculous cures at Lourdes. In peacetime, a yearly average of about 500 doctors visit Lourdes and as many as sixty doctors have been present at the examination of an alleged miracle. The record office of the bureau keeps the case-sheet of those whose cures it has studied, and the certificates brought by the patients from their own doctors are deposited with the reports of the examining doctors at Lourdes. The permanence of the cure is conceded only if the subsequent history of the cure has been recorded for a period of years.

In the second place, the evidence for supernormal cures at Lourdes is of quite a different character from the evidence for alleged "faith cures," such as those claimed by the Christian Scientists. The British Medical Association appointed in 1909 a committee of doctors and clergymen to examine the claims of Christian Science, and this committee reported in 1914 that there was no evidence for the cure of organic diseases.

The Christian Scientists who replied that an unbiased tribute to the effectiveness of cures wrought without medical assistance could hardly be expected from a committee of doctors should refer to the findings of the committee of doctors at Lourdes and to the classic work *Preuves Médicales du Miracle* by Dr. Le Bec, the senior surgeon of a Paris hospital who was president for many years of the Bureau des Constatations. The Rev. F. Woodlock's pamphlet, *The Miracles at Lourdes*, from which the following cases are taken, is a useful summary of the more important cases mentioned by Dr. Le Bec.

Among the more remarkable cures cited by Dr. Le Bec, the following may be cited:

• *Joachine Dehant.* Before she left for Lourdes, Joachine was given a certificate that she was suffering from a dislocated right hip joint, contraction of the tibial muscles so as to produce the effect of a clubfoot, and an ulcer covering two-thirds of the external surface of the right calf. Suppuration was free and the pus extremely foul. The bone was necrosed. Joachine's ulcer was perfectly cured at the second bath; the foot, the hip-joint, and the knee cured on the following day. She weighed four stone three pound on arriving at Lourdes; a few years later she weighed eleven stone ten pound.

• *Mlle. Lebranchu.* Suffering from consumption in the final stage, evening temperatures 102 and 105. Daily blood spitting, and many lung cavities. The girl's condition was elaborately described by Zola, who traveled to Lourdes with her. She is "La Grivotte" of his novel. Zola saw her restored to health after her first bath. Her restoration to health was attested by the declaration of thirty doctors. I have already described Zola's reaction to the miraculous cure of Marie Lemarchand and quoted his characteristic reaction: "Were I to see all the sick at Lourdes cured, I would not believe in a miracle." In his novel, Zola falsifies the facts about Mlle. Lebranchu, for, though he knew that there had been no relapse, his "La Grivotte" has a relapse and dies.

There are over three hundred cases of the cure of consumption in the records of the office. There are many instances of the cure of blindness, full details of which are given in Le Bec's book. A remarkable case reported in the faith-healing issue of the *British Medical Journal* in 1910 is the case of Marie Borel.

• *Marie Borel* arrived at Lourdes after having been confined to bed for thirty months with ankylosed vertebral column, purulent cystitis of the bladder, and six pyostercoral fistulae. For five months the entire waste product of her body passed through these fistulae. In the course of a day at Lourdes these six fistulae closed up spontaneously with no treatment beyond the application, with prayer, of a little spring water. The purulent cystitis of the bladder was cured at the same time.

• *Peter De Rudder* was a Belgian farm laborer whose left leg was shattered in 1867 by the fall of a tree. Seven years passed, and the bones had not united. De Rudder's doctors advised amputation, but De Rudder determined to ask Our Lady of Lourdes, venerated at the shrine of Oostacker, near Ghent, to cure his leg. His doctor, Van Hoestenberghe, who returned to the Faith as a result of the miracle, had given up the case. He testified to De Rudder's condition before the cure in the following words:

I declare on my conscience and on my soul:

1. I have examined De Rudder a dozen times and my last visit was two or three months before the cure.

2. Each time I was able to make the ends of the bones come out of the wound: they were deprived

of their periosteum, there was necrosis, the suppuration was fetid and abundant and has passed
along the tendons. . . .

3. At each examination I introduced two fingers to the bottom of the wound, and always felt a
separation of 4 to 5 centimeters between the broken
parts, and this right across their breadth. I was able
to turn them about easily.

4. A large sequestrum had come away at the
beginning and little bits of bone often came away
during these years.

This testimony was confirmed by witnesses who saw
De Rudder a few days before the cure, and on the way to
Oostacker. The driver of the train on which he traveled to
Oostacker observed the broken leg swinging to and fro
and remarked, "There goes a man who is going to lose
his leg." De Rudder entered the Grotto and began to pray.
Suddenly he felt a strange sensation. He rose, forgetting
his crutches, without which he had not taken a single step
for eight years, knelt before the statue of our Lady, and,
rising unaided, walked three times round the Grotto. He
was cured. He was immediately taken to a neighboring
château. The restored limb was examined; the two wounds
had healed up, leaving two scars. The broken bones had
suddenly been united. There was no shortening of the leg,
in spite of the fact that De Rudder had lost substantial
pieces of bone. The cure was attested by the entire village.

The case was examined and reexamined by various doctors, and the bones, when exhumed, after De Rudder's death, fully support the above history of the case.

Haldane, after reading the Catholic Truth Society pamphlet *A Modern Miracle*, wrote: "I think the odds are that the bones were united, and the septic wounds healed, in a few hours, the most probable alternative being a pious fraud enacted by a large number of people. The only remarkable element in the cure is its speed."

This is much as if someone were to remark, "The only remarkable fact about the Resurrection was that Christ rose from the dead." Medical science can no more explain the *instantaneous* mending of a fracture that had defied doctors for years than the resurrection of a man who has died.

I am concerned for the moment only to establish the *fact* that cures, inexplicable by medical science, have taken place at Lourdes. Cures take place at Lourdes that cannot be explained as the results of "suggestion." Small children and babies, incapable of profiting by "mental" treatment, have been cured at Lourdes of organic diseases, as, for example, the cure of a double clubfoot in a two-year-old child, the miracle occurring as the father, Dr. Aumaitre, held the child's feet in the water. Men have been cured when unconscious or asleep.

The Lourdes water has been analyzed and is ordinary spring water with no radioactivity. Many cures occur without its intervention.

Let me conclude with a quotation from a remarkable book, *Man the Unknown*, which created a sensation in the United States, for Alexis Carrel is one of the most distinguished of modern scientists, a Nobel Prize winner, and one of the more eminent members of the Rockefeller Institute for Medical Research. There are many passages in his book that no convinced Catholic could write, but Carrel is descended from French Catholic stock, and he approaches these problems without the provincial limitations of those scientists who are all influenced by the materialistic fashion of the nineteenth century.

> The author knows, [writes Carrel] that miracles are as far from scientific orthodoxy as mysticity.... But science has to explore the entire field of reality.... He [Carrel] began this study in 1902, at a time when documents were scarce, *when it was difficult for a young doctor, and dangerous for his future career, to become interested in such a subject*....[2]
>
> In all countries, at all times, people have believed in the existence of miracles. . . . But after the great impetus of science during the nineteenth century, such belief completely disappeared. It was generally admitted, not only that miracles did not exist, but that they could not exist. As the laws of

---

[2] *Man the Unknown* (New York: Harper & Bros., 1935), 148, footnote.

thermodynamics make perpetual motion impossible, physiological laws oppose miracles. Such is still the attitude of most physiologists and physicians. However, in view of the facts observed during the last fifty years, this attitude cannot be sustained. The most important cases of miraculous healing have been recorded by the Medical Bureau of Lourdes. Our present conception of the influence of prayer upon pathological lesions is based on the observation of patients who have been cured almost instantaneously of various affections, such as peritoneal tuberculosis, cold abscesses, osteitis, suppurating wounds, lungs, cancer, etc. The process of healing changes little from one individual to another. Often, an acute pain. Then a sudden sensation of being cured. In a few seconds, a few minutes, at the most a few hours, wounds are cicatrized, pathological symptoms disappear, appetite returns. . . . The only condition indispensable to the occurrence of the phenomenon is prayer. *But there is no need for the patient himself to pray, or even to have any religious faith*. It is sufficient that someone around him be in a state of prayer. Such facts are of profound significance. They show the reality of certain relations, of still unknown nature, between psychological and organic processes. They prove the objective importance of the spiritual activities, which hygienists, physicians, educators, and sociologists have almost always neglected to study. They open to man a new world.[3]

"Science," writes Carrel, "has to explore the entire field of reality." "There are few among our ecclesiastics and theologians," writes Dr. Inge, "who would spend five minutes in investigating any alleged supernatural occurrence in our own time. It would be assumed that, if true, it must be ascribed to some obscure natural cause. . . . There is still enough superstition left to win a certain vogue for miraculous cures at Lourdes."

It is interesting to contrast the verdict of the scientists with the verdict of the theologians. Haldane, as we have seen, believes that some of the Lourdes miracles are "possibly true and worth investigating." Alexis Carrel began to investigate them in 1902 and came to the conclusion that many of the Lourdes miracles were genuine. Dr. Inge, who professes great reverence for the scientific method, approves the refusal to "waste five minutes in investigating" an alleged miracle.

---

[3] *Man the Unknown*, 140-150, italics mine.

THREE

The Gospels:
The External Evidence

I N THE FIRST TWO CHAPTERS I have shown:

1. That there is no scientific or philosophic reason that forbids us to believe in miracles.

2. That there exists unimpeachable evidence for certain modern miracles.

It is important to establish the reality of modern miracles, before discussing the evidence for the Resurrection, because the principal obstacle to the universal acceptance of the Resurrection is not any defect in the evidence, but the unconscious or conscious acceptance of a negative dogma: the dogma that miracles do not happen. If there were several cases, universally admitted, of men rising from the dead, no historian would hesitate for one moment to believe that Jesus Christ rose from the dead. And for my part, I am prepared to concede that if the Resurrection were the *only* case of a miracle in all history, I might be tempted to return a verdict of "non proven."

Our next task is to examine the documents that record the Resurrection. Our approach to the problems of authorship and dates must be determined by the exacting standards of scientific history. It is, of course, vain to demand a scientific approach to these problems from those who are determined to reject all facts that conflict with their preconceived dogmas. The pietists of secularism who accept with uncritical faith the basic dogma of their cult, the impossibility of miracles, examine the Gospels not to discover when and by whom they were written but to prove a particular thesis. Miracles do not occur, and therefore any account of a miracle that purports to be by an eyewitness must be a later interpolation.

Of the nineteenth-century critics who adopted this criterion, D.F. Strauss (1808-1874) was the most notorious. His *Life of Jesus for the German People* was published in 1864. That there was nothing supernatural either in the person or in the work of Jesus was the basic principle that Strauss accepted with uncritical faith, "believing where we cannot prove," as Tennyson remarked in a somewhat different connection.

Strauss began life as a Lutheran pastor, and his negative faith in the impossibility of miracles was a form of Lutheranism, "justification by faith" rather than justification by argument. Strauss, indeed, was one of the founders of neo-Lutheranism.

Let us begin our study of the New Testament with the admitted facts that even Strauss does not dispute. "It is certain," writes Strauss, "that, towards the end of the second century, the same four Gospels which we still possess were recognized by the Church, and repeatedly quoted as the writings of those Apostles and of those disciples of the Apostles, whose names they bear, by the three most eminent ecclesiastical teachers—Irenaeus in Gaul, Clement in Alexandria, and Tertullian in Carthage."

Irenaeus, who was Bishop of Lyons about the year A.D. 180, is at great pains to explain why there are exactly four Gospels, no more and no less. The Church extends throughout the whole world, and the world has four quarters. The Gospel is the divine breath, or wind of life, and there are four winds and therefore four Gospels. There is a great deal more to the same effect, but Irenaeus's conviction that the fourfold character of the Gospels was divinely arranged is only of interest to us as decisive evidence for the fact that the pre-eminence of the four Evangelists had been long established when Irenaeus began to write. Strauss himself admits that the *seltsame Beweisführung* (peculiar argument) with which Irenaeus proves the divine necessity for the fourfold character of the Gospel, is evidence of the *vorzüglichen Credit* (outstanding credit) that these four Gospels enjoyed in his day. "It is plain," writes Dr. Salmon, "that the evidence of Irenaeus, even if we had no other, takes us back a long way behind his own time. Books newly come into existence in his time could not have been venerated as he venerated the Gospels. . . . We may fairly conclude that the time of their appearance was beyond then living memory."

In his youth, Irenaeus had known Polycarp, Bishop of Smyrna. "I can recall," he writes in the *Epistle to Florinus*, "the very place where Polycarp used to sit and teach, his manner of speech, his mode of life, his appearance, style of his address to the people, his frequent references to St. John, and to others who had seen our Lord, His miracles, and His teaching; and how, being instructed himself by those who were eye-witnesses of the life of the Word, there was in all he said a strict agreement with the Scriptures." There are critics who affect to believe that St. John's Gospel was written somewhere about 150, but if this were so, what would have been Irenaeus's reaction to so patent a forgery? "No, no!" he would have exclaimed, "this cannot be the work of St. John, for had St. John written a Gospel, my beloved master Polycarp, his disciple, must have known of that Gospel. Polycarp used to repeat from memory the discourses which he had from John, and could not possibly have been silent about a Gospel which would have been St. John's most precious legacy to the Church."

Polycarp died a martyr's death at the age of eighty-six, in the year 155. Had the Fourth Gospel made its first appearance in 150, Polycarp would have rejected it with contempt as an obvious forgery. Irenaeus's unquestioning acceptance of the Fourth Gospel as the work of St. John is plausible only on the assumption that St. John's disciple Polycarp had never questioned the Joannine authorship of the Fourth Gospel.

Within the limits of my space, I can only mention the more important of the many second-century writers who refer to, or who quote from, the four Gospels, such as Justin Martyr, whose *Apology*, written about 150 and addressed to the heathen, contains a summary of the life of our Lord and is full of doctrinal and verbal agreements with St. John. Justin tells his heathen readers that he is quoting from the "memories" of our Lord, known as "Gospels—which were composed by the apostles and by those who followed them." He does not, it is true, mention the names of the authors, but then the heathen whom he was addressing would not be interested in such details.

Tatian, who was Justin's pupil, wrote a harmony of the four Gospels, which he called *Diatessaron*. The earliest extant mention of the names of Matthew and Mark as recognized authors of Gospels is to be found in some fragments of Papias, bishop of Hierapolis early in the second century. It is Papias who is our authority for the fact that Mark was the interpreter of Peter and "wrote down accurately all that he remembered of the things that were either said or done by Christ." Papias also tells us that Matthew "wrote the oracles in Hebrew and each one interpreted them as he could."

Other second-century witnesses of the Gospels are mentioned in the notes on this chapter.

II

The positive arguments for Christianity are more than sufficient to support the Christian conclusion, but it is only when we consider rival theories that the full strength of our case emerges, and for this reason the Christian apologist should never be content merely to *answer* the objections of the skeptic; he should challenge the skeptic to defend his solution. We believe, for instance, that St. John wrote the Fourth Gospel not only because the evidence for his authorship is very strong, but also because no skeptic has ever succeeded in producing a plausible theory to account for the acceptance by the second-century Church of a second-century forgery bearing St. John's name.

The trouble with most skeptics is that they are defective in historical imagination. They approach the problem of the Gospels as if the solution could be found by juggling with texts. They never visualize the conditions under which the Gospels were written and distributed. They never emerge from the valley of the dry bones, and the dry bones of their arguments are never clothed with flesh and blood. They fiddle about with texts, rejecting this passage or that as an "interpolation," but never envisage the "interpolator" as a human being, or produce a plausible theory to account for the success of the "interpolator" in imposing his forgery on the faithful.

You cannot *coerce* belief. Lunacy, as Chesterton points out, has its own watertight logic. The fact that a man is in a lunatic asylum does not disprove his thesis that he is the king of England, for if he were the king of England, the usurper might be tempted to immure him in a lunatic asylum. His explanation fits *some* facts as well as yours, but it fits far fewer facts.

Similarly, there is the faddist who objects that the "Matthew" and "Mark" mentioned by Papias are not necessarily the same works as the Gospels that we now attribute to those apostles. His position is as impregnable to direct assault as would be that of a critic who maintained that the works of Virgil and Horace, referred to by Juvenal—who tells us that these works were in the hands of the schoolboys of his time—were not the works that we now ascribe to those authors. And yet, as Salmon justly says, it would be infinitely easier to alter secular works in private circulation than to effect revolutionary changes in sacred books read Sunday by Sunday in the churches. We are asked to believe not only that the old Gospels which Papias ascribed to Matthew and Mark disappeared without trace, but also that no bishop, presbyter, or layman observed that new Gospels had been substituted in their place. It would be easier to believe that Soviet Russia could have substituted the new national anthem for the old *International* without a single Russian being aware of the change.

The theory of new Gospels substituted for old is not only inherently improbable; it is not supported by a shred of evidence. We know from Eusebius that there was controversy in his time, the first half of the fourth century, about the epistle to the Hebrews and the epistle to the Corinthians, but Eusebius never discusses the authorship of the four Gospels, for the good reason that he had never heard the traditional authorship challenged. The absence of any tradition as to the manner of the first publication of the Gospels is in itself proof of their antiquity, but more impressive—at least to those who see this problem in terms of human beings rather than of manuscripts —is the fact that the missionary activities of the early Church would have been impossible without some authorized record of the life and teaching of Jesus Christ. We know from Justin Martyr's account of the Sunday meetings of Christians that the reading of the story of Jesus Christ was an established tradition at the weekly meetings of the Christians. So long as a Church was presided over by apostles, their personal recollections would suffice, but the first requirement of the elders ordained by the apostles to preside over the churches entrusted to their care was a written and authoritative record of our Lord's life and teaching.

But once we admit the necessity for Gospels in the primitive Church, we have gone a long way to prove that the Gospels which we now possess are the Gospels which were in use in the early years of the Church, for it is impossible to produce a plausible explanation for any substantial alteration of or addition to these Gospels. Nobody has explained how a forger could have obtained credence for a forgery. Theophilus of Antioch, writing about A.D. 180, says: "Writers ought either to have been eyewitnesses

themselves of the things they assert, or at least have accurately learned them from those who had seen them."
"The feeling here expressed is so natural," writes Salmon,

> that I cannot believe that those who were in posses-
> sion of narratives, supposed to have been written
> by men of such rank in the Church as Matthew,
> Mark, and Luke, could allow them to be altered by
> inferior authority. Little do those who suppose such
> an alteration possible know of the conservatism of
> Christian hearers. St. Augustine, in a well-known
> story, tells us that, when a bishop, reading the chap-
> ter about Jonah's gourd, ventured to substitute St.
> Jerome's "hedera" for the established "cucurbita,"
> such a tumult was raised, that if the bishop had
> persevered he would have been left without a con-
> gregation. The feeling that resents such a change
> is due to no later growth of Christian opinion. Try
> the experiment on any child of your acquaintance.
> Tell him a story that interests him; and when next
> you meet him, tell him the story again, making
> variations in your recital, and see whether he will
> not detect the change, and be indignant at it. I
> do not believe, in short, that any Church would
> permit a change to be made in the form of evan-
> gelical instruction in which its members had been
> catechetically trained, unless those who made
> the change were men of authority equal to their

first instructors. . . . If a bishop of the age of Papias had presumed to innovate on the Gospel as it had been delivered by those "which from the beginning were eye-witnesses and ministers of the Word" I venture to say that, like the bishop of whom St. Augustine tells, he would have been left without a congregation.

The skeptic begins his study of the Gospels by making an act of faith in the impossibility of the supernatural. His verdict on the authorship and dates is an unscientific *deduction* from an unproved and false premise. The Christian conclusion is, on the other hand, a scientific *induction* from the facts. The skeptic begins with dogma, the dogma that miracles do not occur, and adjusts the facts to that dogma. The Christian begins with the facts and ends with the dogmas that are alone consistent with and imposed by the facts. The skeptic begins with a prejudgment that miracles do not occur. The Christian ends with the post-judgment that miracles have been proved to occur. The conflict between the Christian and the skeptic is a conflict between post-judice and prejudice.

If it were not for the unscientific prejudice against miracles, nobody would waste time attempting to disprove that the Gospels were written by the apostles and disciples of the apostles whose names they bear. "If we were to apply," writes Salmon, "to the remains of classical literature the same rigour of scrutiny that is used towards the New

Testament, there are but few of them that could stand the test."

The Jesuit Jean Hardouin tried to prove that the *Odes* of Horace and other classical books were written by Benedictine monks in the dark ages, but it would not be easy to refute this theory decisively by producing quotations from the *Odes* by any writer who lived within two centuries of the poet's death, and later testimony would not be thought worth looking at in the case of a New Testament book. "The Roman History of Velleius Paterculus," writes Salmon,

> has come down to us in a single very corrupt manuscript, and the book is only once quoted by Priscian, a grammarian of the sixth century, yet no one entertains the smallest doubt of its genuineness. The first six books of the Annals of Tacitus are also known to us only through a single manuscript which came to light in the fifteenth century. Not long ago an elaborate attempt was made to show that all the books of Annals were forged in that century by an Italian scholar, Poggio. And it was asserted that "no clear and definite allusion to the Annals can be found until the first half of the fifteenth century." The latest editor of the Annals, Mr. Furneaux . . . in answer to the assertion just quoted, can only produce one allusion by no means "clear and definite" and that of a date 300 years later than the historian. . . . where external proof is most abundant in the case of the

profane authors, it falls considerably short of what can be produced in support of the chief books of the New Testament.

That the Gospels were *written* in the fourth century is a popular error due to a confusion between date of *authorship* and date of the earliest complete *manuscripts*.

In the early centuries of our era, manuscripts were still, for the most part, written on papyrus, a frail material compared with vellum, which began to take the place of papyrus in the third century. Fragments of papyrus have been recovered from the dry Egyptian soil, many areas of which are virtually rainless, but hardly a contemporary papyrus survives from Greece, Italy, Gaul, or Spain. There are many other reasons why the earlier papyrus Gospels should have disappeared. A special effort was made by the persecutors of the Church to search for these manuscripts and to destroy them. The Christians themselves, insofar as they were influenced by the expectation of an immediate Second Coming, would have made no special efforts to preserve them for the benefit of posterity. And even in more modern times, the guardians of priceless manuscripts have often been incredibly careless trustees. Thus, we owe the preservation of the famous *Codex Sinaiticus* of the New Testament to pure chance. A German professor, Tischendorf by name, discovered forty-three leaves of an ancient manuscript in a basket full of paper intended for the stove to which the monks of Mount Sinai consigned their debris. Tischendorf obtained these for the asking and secured the rest of the *Codex* some years later.

The case for tradition has been immensely reinforced in recent years by the discovery of the Chester Beatty Biblical Papyri in 1930. The papyri, found in a Coptic graveyard, enclosed in one or more jars, near the Nile, include fragments of the Gospels, written in a small hand which paleographers assign to the first half of the third century. More recently, a small fragment of a papyrus codex containing parts of St. John 18: 31-33, 37, 38 was discovered by Mr. C.H. Roberts among the papyri in the John Rylands Library at Manchester. Paleographers assign this fragment to the *first half of the second century*, a conclusive proof of the early date of the Fourth Gospel, a Gospel which, as we shall see, has been the object of sustained attack. Sir Frederic Kenyon of the British Museum sums up the result of these discoveries in his book *The Story of the Bible*:

> It will now be realized what an epoch-making addition to our knowledge of the history of the Bible has been made by this discovery. Instead of our evidence for the text of the Greek Bible beginning with the fourth century we now have several witnesses from the third century, and one even from the beginning of the second. . . .
>
> For all the works of classical antiquity we have to depend on manuscripts written long after their original composition. The author who is in the best

case in this respect is Virgil, yet the earliest manuscript of Virgil that we now possess was written some 350 years after his death. For all other classical writers, the interval between the date of the author and the earliest extant manuscript of his works is much greater. For Livy it is about 500 years, for Horace 900, for most of Plato 1,300, for Euripides 1,600. On the other hand the great vellum uncials of the New Testament were written perhaps some 250 years after the date when the Gospels were actually composed, while we now have papyrus manuscripts which reduce the interval by a hundred years. And while the manuscripts of any classical author amount at most to a few score, and in some cases only to a few units, the manuscripts of the Bible are reckoned by thousands.

The case for the traditional authorship and dates of the four Gospels is indeed so overwhelmingly strong that there would be little scope for controversy but for the fact that the Gospels record miracles.

Had the Rylands fragment been discovered a century ago, we would have been spared libraries of books, all of which can now be relegated to the limbo of exploded theories. Père F.M. Braun, O.P., reminds us that shortly before these papyrus fragments were discovered, Loisy had decided that the Fourth Gospel was written between 135 and 140 and that Couchod had suggested A.D. 150 as the date when St. Luke's Gospel was written. Père Lagrange, writing in 1936 in *La Revue Biblique*, remarked drily that critics such as these were not able to withstand "even the shock of a tiny fragment of papyrus."

FOUR

The Gospels:
The Internal Evidence

NO RESPONSIBLE CRITIC MAINTAINS that the Gospels are the work of eyewitnesses who deliberately set down what they knew to be untrue. Those who reject the miraculous element in the Gospels maintain either that the Gospels were written by eyewitnesses who mistook for miracles phenomena that were capable of a natural explanation or that the Gospels were written many years after the events they described by men who were not eyewitnesses of those events. Heinrich Paulus (1761-1851) adopted the former hypothesis in his *Life of Christ*, published in 1828. There was nothing, he insists, miraculous about the feeding of the five thousand. A lot of greedy people had concealed their own stores of food but were shamed into sharing them with their hungry neighbors when Christ and the apostles began to distribute their own scanty supplies. Again, our Lord *seemed* to walk on the water, but this was an optical illusion, for, in fact, he was walking on the bank.

Strauss was too intelligent to be impressed by such puerilities. "If the Gospels," he writes, "are genuine historical sources, it is impossible to eliminate the miraculous from the life of Jesus." And consequently Strauss maintained that the Gospels were legendary accounts put together many years after the events they purported to describe.

If the Gospels are mainly fictitious, with a small substratum of fact overlaid by legend, it is difficult to explain the success of the evangelists in creating a character who lives as no character in fiction lives. It is only the greatest of dramatists and novelists who can create such characters as Odysseus, Dido, Hamlet, and Don Quixote with a universal appeal transcending the limitations of the author's age and of the author's nation; but no character, in ancient or in modern literature, has the same timeless universal appeal as Jesus. It is strange that creative genius such as this should have left no other mark in the literature of the age. Why, for instance, are the parables, if the parables are fictitious, unique? Why was the knack of inventing such discourses confined to this small group of writers? Ernest Renan, who rejects as unreliable the Gospel record of what our Lord *did*, accepts as trustworthy the report of what our Lord *said*. He speaks of the "naturalness, the ineffable truth, the matchless charm of the Synoptic discourses;

their profound Hebrew turn; the analogies they present to the sayings of the Jewish doctors of the same time; their perfect harmony with the scenery of Galilee. . . . A kind of brilliance, a divine force, underlines these words, if I may say so, detaches them from the context, and enables the critic easily to recognize them. The true words of Jesus, so to say, reveal themselves. When they are touched in this chaos of traditions of unequal authenticity we feel them vibrate."

Now, if these discourses had been invented, similar discourses could have been invented. "Actually, it is," as Salmon remarks, "a little surprising that the men who were so deeply impressed by our Lord's teaching, and who so fully imbibed the spirit of it, should never have attempted to imitate its form. In point of style we travel into a new country when we pass from the Synoptic Gospels and to the Apostolic Epistles. . . . Among early uninspired Christian writers there were several imitators of the Apostolic Epistles, but only one, Hermas, who attempted to imitate the parables, and that with such poor success that we need the less wonder that others did not try the experiment."

Not enough has been made of the fantastic contrast between the New Testament and the Apocryphal New Testament. It is a pity that the anti-miraculists who assert that this or that Gospel was forged in the second century are not confronted more frequently with the second-century forgeries purporting to be the work of the apostles. "Among the prayers and the discourses of the apostles," writes Dr. Montague James in his preface to *The Apocryphal New Testament*, "in the spurious Acts some utterances may be found which are remarkable and even beautiful . . . but the authors do not speak with the voices of Paul or of John, or with the quiet simplicity of the first three Gospels. It is not unfair to say that when they attempt the former tone they are theatrical, and when they essay the latter they are jejune."

The contrast between the discourses of our Lord that we know to have been invented and the discourses recorded in the Gospels compels even anti-miraculists like Renan to accept the latter as genuine records of what our Lord said.

Now, records of conversation that carry conviction are not very common. Samuel Johnson's table talk survives because James Boswell kept a careful and contemporary record of what Johnson said. Johann Goethe's table talk has been preserved because Johann Eckermann was Boswellian in his methods. I can speak from personal experience on the contrast between conversation recorded at the time and conversation recorded in later years. When I was a boy, I was puzzled by the contrast between the conversation of boys as recorded in school stories and the actual conversation of my friends. I came to the conclusion that these school stories were written by adults who had forgotten how they themselves talked as boys, and I decided to keep a careful record of the conversation of my contemporaries

as the basis for a school story that I proposed to write when
I left school. An American author, Mr. Edward Mack, in a
two-volume study of the public school system (published
by Columbia University Press) has described my book *The
Harrovians* as "the inauguration of a new type of fiction,"
but the book owed such merits as it possessed to the efforts I made as a boy to record conversation within a few
hours of the conversation's taking place. In a more recent
book, I tried to give some impression of the table talk of a
most brilliant conversationalist, but because I had taken no
notes at the time, I could remember only a few *bon mots*,
and my attempt ended in failure.

All those who, like Renan and many of the anti-miraculists, accept as genuine the record of our Lord's discourses and reject as spurious the record of his miracles
are committed to the unlikely hypothesis that the apostles
were surprisingly accurate as ear-witnesses and hopelessly
inaccurate as eyewitnesses, but this is contrary to all human experience, for reports of what was seen are almost
invariably more accurate than reports of what was said.
Accurate ear-witnesses are far less common than accurate
eyewitnesses. If we maintain that the evangelists should
be believed when they report what our Lord *said*, we are
compelled to accept one of the following three hypotheses:

1. One or more of the apostles wrote down the discourses of our Lord at the time they were delivered
or shortly afterward.

2. The evangelists were aided by supernatural inspiration.

3. The discourses were invented by the evangelists.

The first and second of these hypotheses are not mutually exclusive, but the second (supernatural inspiration) is not admissible *at this stage of our inquiry*, for the documents on which we base our belief in the Resurrection must be examined and must be proved to be reliable by the exacting standards of scientific history before we can even begin to speculate on the possibility of inspiration.

If we reject the first two hypotheses and defend the only remaining possibility, that the Gospels are works of fiction, there is no reason why the Gospel of St. Matthew should be more convincing than the admittedly fictitious Gospel of Pseudo-Matthew, and on this hypothesis it is difficult to explain the contrast between the sayings of Jesus as recorded by St. Matthew and the sayings of Jesus as recorded by the Pseudo-Matthew. Let us test this theory by comparing the following passage from St. Matthew:

> Consider the lilies of the field, how they grow; they neither toil nor spin; yet I tell you, even Solomon in all his glory was not arrayed like one of these. But if God so clothes the grass of the field, which today is alive and tomorrow is thrown into the oven, will he not much more clothe you, O men of little faith? (Matt. 6:28-30).

. . . with the following passage from Pseudo-Matthew:

Jesus went to school the second time. "Say Alpha."
Jesus: "Tell thou me first what Beta is, and I will
tell thee what Alpha is." The master smote him and
died.

Jesus (to his parents): "What you say is well enough
for ordinary people. I have no earthly father. When
I am lifted up from earth I will make all mention
of your descent to cease. I know when you were
born and how long you have to live." All cried out
in wonder. "We have never heard the like." Jesus:
"Does this surprise you? I will tell you more. I have
seen Abraham."

Even more striking is the contrast between the miracles of the Gospels and the miracles described by this
Pseudo-Matthew.

When Jesus was in Galilee at the beginning of his
fourth year, he was playing by the Jordan, and made
seven pools. A boy spoiled them and was struck
dead. The parents complained. Joseph asked Mary
to admonish Jesus. She begged him not to do such
things and he, not willing to grieve her, smote the
backside of the dead boy with his foot and bade him
rise, which he did, and Jesus went on with his pools.
Jesus took clay from the pools and made twelve
sparrows on the sabbath. A Jew saw it and spoke to

Joseph, who spoke to Jesus. Jesus clapped his hands and bade the sparrows fly away. All marveled, and some went and told the Chief Priests and Pharisees. The son of Annas broke up the pools with a stick and Jesus with a word withered him up.

The Jesus of Pseudo-Matthew is a mere magician. The vulgar marvels he performs are unredeemed by beauty, have no relevance to character and no organic relationship to environment. They are nothing more than crude manifestations of vindictive and arrogant power, but in the Gospels the miraculous element is interwoven into the very texture of human stories that carry complete conviction. "Christ's miracles," as Bishop Gore remarks, "were incidental, and issued from a pity that knew that it had power to heal men's sickness and to supply their physical needs, and could not refrain from using it." And again and again, these miracles give occasion for sayings and gestures of Christ that bear the hallmark of authenticity.

Whereas neither the Jesus of the apocryphal Gospels nor the minor characters ever come to life, least of all in the miracle scenes, the characterization in the Gospel miracles is masterly.

Reread, for instance, St. John's account of the restoration of sight to the man who was born blind (John 9). There is not a character in this story who is not true to type. The disciples, the neighbors, the parents of the blind man, the Pharisees, and the blind man himself all act and speak exactly as we would expect them to act and speak, so much so that the intimate knowledge displayed by the writer of the first-century Jew has been cited by that distinguished Biblical scholar, the late Dr. William Sanday, as conclusive evidence against the theory that the Gospel was the work of a second-century Christian: "As he passed by, he saw a man blind from his birth. And his disciples asked him, 'Rabbi, who sinned, this man or his parents, that he was born blind?' Jesus answered, 'It was not that this man sinned, or his parents, but that the works of God might be made manifest in him'" (John 9:1-3).

> Notice [writes Dr. Sanday] in this connection the following essentially Jewish ideas, the connection of sin with physical infirmity, and the speculation as to how far back, in a particular case, the connection went—whether it was confined to the individual affected himself, or whether it went back to his parents; the observance of the sabbath as indispensable to one who had a divine mission; in reply to this, the plea that none but a righteous man could work miracles; the relation of discipleship, and the claim of the Pharisees to be in the strict sense Moses' disciples; and finally the characteristic abuse of one who bore in his body the mark of having been born in sin, and yet presumed to teach doctors of the Law; for such a one expulsion from the synagogue was a fitting penalty.

It is so much easier to blame the sufferer than to sympathize with suffering. There has never been a persecution of Christians from the first to the twentieth century without the question being asked, "Who sinned?" and without many people attempting to answer that it is the persecuted who have sinned. The neighbors are mildly interested and no more. And, of course, their first instinct is to explain away the miracle. It's all a case of mistaken identity. "Some said, 'It is he'; others said, 'No, but he is like him.' He said, 'I am the man.'

"They said to him, 'Then how were your eyes opened?' He answered, 'The man called Jesus made clay and anointed my eyes and said to me, "Go to Siloam and wash"; so I went and washed and received my sight'" (John 9:9-11).

The neighbors agree that this is a case for the authorities, so the man who was blind is brought before the Pharisees and repeats his story. "Some of the Pharisees said, 'This man is not from God, for he does not keep the sabbath.' But others said, 'How can a man who is a sinner do such signs?' There was a division among them" (John 9:16).

But it is, of course, only a minority who are open to conviction, and the majority still hope that this dubious miracle may turn out to be a mare's nest. . . . These beggars are capable of anything. . . . How do we know this is really the man who was blind? So they send for the parents of the man who was born blind, humble people who prefer to be left undisturbed in their obscurity, and who dread the limelight. They cannot deny their parentage but they refuse to commit themselves to any explanation of facts which they are forced to concede. So they disclaim responsibility and pass up these awkward questions to their son.

"'We know that this is our son, and that he was born blind; but how he now sees we do not know, nor do we know who opened his eyes. Ask him; he is of age, he will speak for himself.' His parents said this because they feared the Jews, for the Jews had already agreed that if any one should confess him to be Christ, he was to be put out of the synagogue. Therefore his parents said, 'He is of age, ask him'" (John 9:20-23). The man who was blind is no hero. Like his parents, he fears the Jews, and like his parents, he tries to stick rigidly to the facts and to avoid their controversial complications.

"So for the second time they called the man who had been blind, and said to him, 'Give God the praise; we know that this man is a sinner.' He answered, 'Whether he is a sinner, I do not know; one thing I know, that though I was blind, now I see'" (John 9:24-25).

The Pharisees fall back on that favorite device of cross-examiners: the reiterated question—"What did he do to you? How did he open your eyes?" The man who was blind loses his patience, and with anger comes courage. "He answered them, 'I have told you already, and you would not listen. Why do you want to hear it again? Do you too want to become his disciples?'" Temper is rising on both sides: "And they reviled him, saying, 'You are his disciple, but we are disciples of Moses. We know that God has spoken to Moses, but as for this man, we do not know where he comes from.'" And now at last the man who was born blind has to make up his own mind about the character and motives of his benefactor. His instinctive loyalties overcome his fears, and he is provoked by an attack on him who healed him into an uncompromising defense of Jesus. "Why, this is a marvel!" he answers with splendid irony. "'You do not know where he comes from, and yet he opened my eyes. We know that God does not listen to sinners, but if any one is a worshiper of God and does his will, God listens to him. Never since the world began has it been heard that any one opened the eyes of a man born blind. If this man were not from God, he could do nothing.' They answered him, 'You were born in utter sin, and would you teach us?' And they cast him out." And Jesus hearing "that they had cast him out" went in search of him, "and having found him he said, 'Do you believe in the Son of man?' He answered, 'And who is he, sir, that I may believe in him?' Jesus said to him, 'You have seen him, and it is he who speaks to you.' He said, 'Lord, I believe'; and he worshiped him" (John 9:26-38).

The man who was born blind is the prototype of converts who are neither credulous nor skeptical, ordinary folk who do not jump rashly to conclusions but who advance cautiously from one demonstrated fact to another. He holds on firmly to the central fact: "One thing I know that whereas I was blind, now I see," and from this great premise he slowly, very slowly, proceeds to the inevitable

conclusions. The man who healed him must be as wonderful as his works. And how subtly St. John describes the
slow hesitating advance from agnosticism to faith. "If he be
a sinner I know not. . . . Unless this man were of God he
could do nothing. . . . Who is he, Lord, that I may believe in
him? . . . And falling down, he adored him." Everything in
this story rings true, the conversation, the characterization
of disciples, neighbors, parents, Pharisees, and above all of
the man himself. Even the minor details are convincing,
for what forger would have invented the mixture of clay
and spittle as the mode of healing? And so once again we
are forced back to reexamine our premises. Whatever else
may be the true origin of the story, it did not originate
in the confusion between a natural phenomenon and a
miracle. All were agreed, parents and neighbors, that the
man had been born blind. Paulus's theory (see earlier)
does not fit this case.

Did St. John invent it? Did the disciples conspire to
impose upon the world the myth of a wonder-working
Savior? The question often asked by Roman lawyers—*Cui
bono?*—was never more relevant. "To whom was it for a
good?" Who would have profited by such a deception? Not
the disciples who faced martyrdom in defense of their faith
in one who proved his claim to be God by the miracles
he worked. Even the underworld of atheism hesitates to
accuse the disciples of conscious fraud.

But perhaps these miracles are later interpolations?
This hypothesis would be plausible if we could detect any

stylistic or other differences between the passages describing miracles and the rest of the text. But this is not the case. Remove these passages and the amputated text is as lifeless as a body from which the heart has been removed. The unity of the Fourth Gospel is so striking that even Strauss conceded that the book was "woven without seam." No, there are only two hypotheses we need to consider. Either the Gospels are the works of eyewitnesses who truthfully recorded genuine miracles, or they are works of fiction.

There is nothing inherently improbable in a legendary figure inspiring one masterpiece, and if only one Gospel had survived, the theory that this Gospel was a masterpiece of imaginative writing might be tenable, but it is difficult to believe that we are indebted for no fewer than four masterpieces to a mere handful of contemporaries, of whom two belonged to the small group of immediate disciples and two to those in immediate touch with the Twelve.

Every critic concedes to the evangelists a genius for characterization. Now, the power to describe character, I will not say with genius but even with a fair ability, is comparatively rare. Watch a young man in love trying to convey the personality of the object of his affections. Unless he is an exceptional young man, he will rely exclusively on labels—"divine" . . . "enchanting" . . . "perfect complexion" . . . "such good company," etc.—but the young woman never comes alive, and nothing emerges from this mist of descriptive adjectives but the fact that he is very much in love. Again, how often have we heard people try and fail to convey the atmosphere of a riotous party. "Old Bob was in topping form. He was screamingly funny. What did he say? Oh, I can't remember, but he was a scream. You'd have roared with laughter if you had been there." Perhaps . . . *if* we had been there.

The experienced novelist never *labels* his characters. He shows them in action. By witty dialogue he conveys the character of a wit, by brave action of a hero. There are no labels in the Gospels. The evangelists do not describe Christ. They tell us what he did, and they tell us what he said. They add no word of praise when they write of Christ and no word of blame when they describe the betrayal or the denial. In our own times, writers have dredged the dictionaries in search of epithets to label traitors in the service of Hitler, but nothing written of Vidkun Quisling and his tribe is as effective as the few words in which St. John introduces Judas: "But Judas Iscariot, one of his disciples (he who was to betray him), said, 'Why was this ointment not sold for three hundred denarii and given to the poor?' This he said, not that he cared for the poor but because he was a thief, and as he had the money box he used to take what was put into it" (John 12:4-6). And nothing could be simpler or more telling than the words in which St. John describes the traitor's exit from the last supper: "So, after receiving the morsel, he immediately went out; *and it was night*" (John 13:30). Every word evokes a picture. The door opens, the silhouetted traitor shows up against the stars, and Judas passes out into the darkness.

There is no more exactive test for a fiction writer than the problem of combining art and propaganda. There is no necessary inconsistency between propaganda and art, for propaganda merely means things that ought to be propagated and such things may be propagated in words or in song, in paint or in stone. Chartres for instance is Catholic propaganda in stone, Omar Khayam skeptical propaganda in verse. But though many fine propaganda novels have been written, nowhere is poor technique more fatal than in a propaganda novel to the illusion that the novelist seeks to convey, and nothing is more tedious than the dialogue that reads not like conversation between different people but like a religious or political essay by the writer, cut into small sections, and distributed at random to different characters.

Gospel means "good news," and it was to propagate the good news of God that the Gospels were written. It is the paradox of the Gospels that the loveliness which is the note of all great art was the unintended byproduct of the work of men who were interested *only* in propaganda.

If, however, we are to judge the Gospels by the criterion of fiction, we have to account for the curious fact that works which in many respects compare favorably with the supreme masterpieces of all, in other respects violate rules that even unpracticed writers invariably observe. The infallibility of the author is a basic convention of imaginative fiction. Loose ends and unsolved conundrums are intolerable in a novel. The evangelists, on the other hand, leave many things that perplex us unexplained because they themselves did not know the explanation. Indeed, they are so preoccupied with the central theme that they sometimes provide no clues even to mysteries to which they knew the answer. St. Mark, for instance, describes the young man who followed as Christ was being led away from the garden of Gethsemane: "And a young man followed him, with nothing but a linen cloth about his body; and they seized him, but he left the linen cloth and ran away naked" (Mark 14:51-52). A modern biographer who recorded so strange an incident would, at least, speculate about the identity of this young man and offer some tentative explanation of his curiously inadequate wardrobe, but St. Mark who, according to tradition, was the young man in question, throws no beam of light across the darkness into which the young man fled.

It is, indeed, not only in the little details that he records but in the details that he unaccountably fails to record that the eyewitness is differentiated from the realistic writer of fiction. The Gospels are full of gaps that a fiction writer would have filled in. The story of the woman taken in adultery would be one of the most perfect short stories in fiction but for one striking omission. Tolstoy, had he been capable of writing such a story, and of inventing that sublime touch, Jesus stooping down and writing on the ground, as though he heard them not, could never have resisted telling us *what* Jesus wrote. St. John, who is not writing fiction, describes only what he saw, and he may have been prevented from seeing what Christ wrote for any one of many reasons. The Pharisees were crowding around Jesus, and John may have been on the outskirts of the crowd, or his whole attention may have been focused on the woman whose fate was in suspense.

It is easy to explain the omissions of those who described only what they saw and what they remembered, but no fiction writer capable of inventing so sublime a story could have resisted rounding it off by representing our Lord as writing something very telling in the dust, something very telling indeed, but infinitely less telling than the silence of St. John.

FIVE

The Vindication of St. Luke

I N 1879 A STUDENTSHIP OF £300 a year for three years
was instituted in the University of Oxford for travel and
research in Greece and Asia Minor. There were two candidates. One was a brilliant young man who had graduated
from Trinity College, Dublin, and had dazzled Oxford
with his brilliance. He had taken first-class honors with
less work than any undergraduate within the memory of
man. The other candidate was a Scot who had graduated
from Aberdeen and then taken a scholarship at Oxford.
His name was Ramsay, later Sir William Ramsay, to whose
vindication of St. Luke reference has already been made in
the introduction. The electors could not come to a decision
between the Irishman and the Scot. "Sir Charles Newton,"
writes Ramsay, "remarked that it would be necessary to

hold an examination to decide. 'In that case,' I replied, 'I am not a candidate.' He asked the reason. I said I had long resolved that I would not compete against men junior to myself and also that I did not like the examination system. 'But,' he replied, 'what is to be done when two candidates are nearly equal? How are we to decide?' 'If you have any doubt, prefer the junior man.'" In spite of, or perhaps because of this cavalier attitude to those in whose hands his fate lay, William Ramsay was elected to the studentship. Never was an award more triumphantly vindicated. Ramsay went to Asia Minor, and in the course of the next thirty-four years made his reputation as one of the world's greatest authorities on the regions he explored. The defeated candidate, after a brilliant social and literary career in London went to Reading jail and died in exile. His name was Oscar Wilde.

Ramsay, in his famous book *The Bearing of Recent Discovery on the Trustworthiness of the New Testament*, tells us that he began to prepare for his life work by reading every available book describing journeys in Asia Minor, among others, the Acts of the Apostles:

> I began to do so without expecting any information of value regarding the condition of Asia Minor at the time when Paul was living. I had read a good deal of modern criticism about the book, and dutifully accepted the current opinion that it was written during the second half of the second century

by an author who wished to influence the minds of people in his own time by a highly wrought and imaginative description of the early Church. His object was not to present a trustworthy picture of facts in the period about A.D. 50, but to produce a certain effect on his own time by setting forth a carefully coloured account of events and persons of that older period. He wrote for his contemporaries, not for truth.

The first change of judgment was provoked by a point of geography. Critics were unanimous in stating that St. Luke had blundered badly by writing as if Iconium was not in Lycaonia. Ramsay's discoveries in Asia Minor confirmed in every detail the accuracy of the Lucan geography. Moreover he proved that where St. Luke differed from his modern critics in intricate details of local government in the Roman Empire, St. Luke was invariably right and his critics invariably wrong.

At Thessalonica, for instance, the magistrates are called politarchs. Now, there is no ancient author who uses this name in connection with Thessalonica, and consequently St. Luke's use of the word was cited by hostile critics as an example of his inaccuracy. His critics were unaware that an old arch at the modern Salonika bore an inscription that it had been raised by seven politarchs. Once again, modern discovery had vindicated the ancient author against modern critics. Again, St. Luke's description of the ruler at

Cyprus as proconsul was once denounced as a mistake and is now admitted to be accurate. Herod Agrippa I, shortly before his death is described as *king;* we now know that he held this title for the last three years of his government, though there had been no king in Judea for the previous thirty years, nor for many centuries afterward. Equally correct is the title of governor or procurator applied to both Felix and Festus.

That Acts contained and described a series of improbable incidents was a view that has not been tenable or possible since 1890 except through total disregard of recent advance in knowledge. It had by that time become evident that every incident described in Acts is just what might be expected in ancient surroundings. The officials with whom Paul and his companions were brought in contact are those who would be there. Every person is found just where he ought to be: proconsuls in senatorial provinces, asiarchs in Ephesus, strategoi in Philippi, politarchs in Thessalonica, magicians and soothsayers everywhere. The difficulties which the Apostles encountered were such as they must inevitably meet in ancient society. The magistrates take action against them in a strictly managed Roman colony like Pisidian Antioch or Philippi, where legality and order reigned; riotous crowds try to take the law into their own hands in the less strictly governed Hellenistic or Hellenic cities like Iconium and Ephesus and Thessalonica. Lystra is an exceptional case; but in Lystra the Roman element was weak from the beginning and quickly melted into the older population. Yet how differently does the catastrophe proceed in Antioch and in Philippi, or in Iconium and Thessalonica and Ephesus. The variety is endless, as real life is infinitely varied. A work composed in late time for hortatory purposes would have no such variety, and no such local truth.

Legal proceedings are taken against Paul and his friends in many places, and accusations have to be made in each case according to the forms of the Roman law. The accusation varies in each case; it is nowhere the same as in any other city; yet it is everywhere in accordance with Roman forms.

There is one delicacy of terminology—so delicate that it has never been sufficiently noted—which characterises the language of Acts. We are too apt to think and speak of the population in all those Anatolian cities as Hellenes, when we desire to speak accurately; but that is really inaccurate. There was a certain generic character in the population of those cities, if we set aside the Italians, i.e., Roman citizens; but in a Roman colony this native population was the *plebs* (*ohclos* in Greek), while in a Hellenistic city like Iconium it was called the Hellenes. Luke is right in this: he uses *ochlos* ("multitude") at Antioch and Lystra, but Hellenes at Iconium.

Further study of Acts, 13-21, showed that the book could bear the most minute scrutiny as an authority for the facts of the Aegean world, and that it was written with such judgement, skill, art, and perception of truth as to be a model of historical statement. It is marvellously concise and yet marvellously lucid. . . .

The more I have studied the narrative of Acts, and the more I have learned year after year about Graeco-Roman society and thoughts and fashions, and organization in those provinces, the more I admire and the better I understand. I set out to look for truth on the borderland where Greece and Asia meet, and found it here. You may press the words of Luke in a degree far beyond any other historian's, and they stand the keenest scrutiny and the hardest treatment.

Ramsay, as we have seen, began his work strongly prejudiced against Acts. As he remarks in his book *St. Paul, The Traveller and the Roman Citizen*: "The ingenuity and apparent completeness of the Tübingen theory had at one time completely convinced me," but long before he had completed his research, he came to the conclusion that Acts is one of the most reliable of authorities for the state of the Roman Empire in the first century and that he was fully justified in "placing the author of Acts among the historians of the first rank."

Long before Ramsay began his research, critics of all schools had recognized that the so-called "we" sections— that is, the section in which St. Luke writes in the first person plural—were almost certainly the works of eye-witnesses. Thus, Dr. S. Davidson, the author of a well-known *Introduction to the New Testament*, in which the anti-miraculist position is adopted, writes of these "we" sections that they are "characterized by a circumstantiality of detail, a vividness of description, an exact knowledge of localities, an acquaintance with the phrases and habits of seamen, which betray one who was personally present."

A scientific critic would begin by comparing the "we" sections with the rest of Acts. If he could find no stylistic differences between the "we" sections and the rest, he would accept, if only as a working hypothesis, the fact that Acts was the work of a single author. The anti-miraculist is more concerned to prove his basic dogma than to discover the truth. He starts from the assumption that as much as possible of the New Testament has to be proved to be spurious and that as little as possible must be conceded to be the work of eyewitnesses. If forced to concede the genuineness of eyewitness authorship of any part of the New Testament, he abandons just so much of his theory as he can no longer defend and clings with even greater tenacity to the rest.

The anti-miraculist seems to assume that he is dispensed from the obligations binding on all other historians, the obligation to support his arguments with proof. If he is asked to choose between two hypotheses of which the first is in accord with Christian tradition and also supported by evidence, and the second is in accord with the anti-miraculist hypothesis and unsupported by any evidence, he instinctively chooses the latter. Thus, the critics of the Tübingen school *assumed* that a second-century compiler *happened* to secure the memoranda really made by a traveling companion of St. Paul, that this compiler, whose name we did not know and for whose existence *no* evidence is produced, worked these memoranda into a narrative, mainly fictitious, and intended to popularize the writer's tendentious views about the early Church. No attempt is made, as Salmon points out, to explain how

an unknown person in the second century got exclusive possession of some of the most precious relics of the Apostolic age—relics the authenticity of which is proved by internal evidence, and yet of which no one but this compiler seems ever to have heard—while the compiler himself vanished out of knowledge. The rationalist critics would scarcely make their story more miraculous if they presented their legend in the form, that the "we" sections were brought to Rome by an angel from heaven, who immediately after disappeared. But new difficulties arise when they try to tear the "we" sections away from the rest of Acts; for this book is not one of those low organizations which do not resent being pulled asunder. It is on the contrary a highly organised structure, showing evident marks that the whole proceeded from a single author. Thus references, direct or implied, are repeatedly made from one part of the book to another.

In his book *The Medical Language of St. Luke*, Dr. Hobart has proved the perfect unity of authorship throughout the whole of the Third Gospel and Acts. Such slight differences between one part of the Lucan writings and another are, as Ramsay remarks, "a mere trifle in comparison with the complete identity in language, vocabulary, intentions, interests and method of narration" *(Luke, the Physician,* p. 7).

The anti-miraculist Davidson concedes that these linguistic resemblances are very striking and, with the tenacity of the anti-miraculist, falls back on a new hypothesis. "It is clear that the writer of the book was not a mere compiler but an author," an author who worked up his material into a homogeneous whole. But this theory raises new difficulties, for if we are expected to accept the hypothesis of a second-century compiler who worked his heterogeneous materials into an artistic unity with consummate skill we may ask why the join-ups between the "we" sections and the rest of *Acts* are so inartistic. These sudden transitions, which are natural enough on the assumption that St. Luke wrote the whole book, are curiously clumsy on the assumption that the book is the work of more than one author. But it is difficult to credit this hypothetical second-century compiler with the contempt for artistry that these clumsy join-ups seem to exhibit (on the assumption and only on the assumption that the different sections so clumsily woven together are by different authors), for it is not easy to convict him of literary ineptitude. Take the letter of Claudius Lysias in Acts. If we are not to believe that this was the real letter the chief captain sent, what dramatic skill it required to have invented it, making the chief captain, by a gentle distortion of the facts, give them the coloring which sets his own conduct in the most favorable light. There is the same dramatic propriety in the exordium of Tertullus, the hearing before Agrippa, the proceedings before Gallio; or, to go back still earlier, in the story of Peter knocking at the door, and Rhoda so delighted that she runs off with the news without waiting to open to him. A critic must be destitute of the most elementary qualifications for his art who does not perceive that the writer of Acts is no uneducated clumsy patcher together of documents, but a literary artist who thoroughly understands how to tell a story.

The determination of anti-miraculists to assign as late a date as possible to Acts is mainly inspired by the anxiety to discredit the Third Gospel, for the great majority of anti-miraculists concede that the author of St. Luke and the author (or compiler) of Acts are one and the same person. "One need not," wrote Renan, "waste time proving a proposition which has never been seriously contested."

If, then, we can show that Acts was written by a close traveling companion of St. Paul, it follows that the Third Gospel must also be the work of somebody in close contact with eyewitnesses of the events described, and if this is admitted, it is very difficult, or even as Strauss maintained, "impossible to eliminate the miraculous from the life of Jesus."

It was, therefore, vital to the position of the anti-miraculists to refute Ramsay's vindication of Luke as a historian. A distinguished reviewer of Ramsay's *St. Paul the Traveller* ended his review with the words, "If Luke is a great historian, what would the author of this book make of Luke 2, 1-3?" Nothing more was needed, for this brief question was deemed sufficient.

Msgr. Knox's translation of these verses is as follows: "It happened that a decree went out at this time from the Emperor Augustus, enjoining that the whole world should be registered.[4] This register was the one first made during the time when Cyrinus[5] was governor of Syria. All must go and give in their names each in their own city."

---

[4] "Registered": The Douay-Rheims version has "enrolled." Both Knox and the Douay are more accurate than the "taxed" of the Authorized Version (A.V.).

[5] Cyrenius (A.V.).

St. Luke in this chapter makes five statements, all of which were rejected by the anti-miraculist critics as demonstrably false, all of which have since proved to be true. These statements are:

- that Cyrinus was governor when Joseph was alleged to have gone to Bethlehem, for the date of this journey must have been, according to St. Luke, before Herod died and Cyrinus, according to the critics, was never Governor of Syria during Herod's lifetime;

- that Augustus issued a decree ordering a census;

- that there was a regular system of census under the empire;

- that the head of the household had to return to his original home to be registered;

- that the head of the household had to be accompanied by his wife.

On *all* these points Luke has been proved to be right and his critics wrong. His vindication is partly the result of recent discoveries in Egypt of census papers that had been preserved in the dry soil and partly the result of Ramsay's explorations in Asia Minor. "In every case," writes Ramsay, "that has been sufficiently tested, Luke has been proved to state, not merely correctly in a superficial and external fashion, but correctly with insight and fine historic sense, the facts of history and of Roman organization in municipal and provincial and imperial government. Such progress as the present writer has been enabled to make in discovery is largely due to the early appreciation of the fact that Luke is a safe guide. . . . Nowhere in the whole range of historical study has there ever been such a complete revolution of opinion."

And what, you may ask, was the effect on the anti-miraculist? Ulrich Wilcken, who collaborated with Ludwig Mitteis in a study of the papyri found in Egypt *(Papyruskunde)*, is a stubborn anti-miraculist and therefore constrained to reconcile the now-admitted accuracy of Luke on these contested points, with his determination to believe that the story of the Nativity was unadulterated legend. He argues that Luke, who was thoroughly familiar with the census regulations, gave verisimilitude to his legend by providing it with a historical framework. He correctly infers from a passage in the London papyri that the entire population had to present themselves personally for inspection. "Accordingly," he writes, "Joseph and Mary in the legend of Luke must both go to Bethlehem." It is, however, as Ramsay drily remarks, "contrary to every canon of historical criticism that the story should be set aside as a legend because all the details in it are true. . . . Luke's narrative used to be called a legend, because it was historically false. Now it is called by Wilcken a legend because every detail has been demonstrated to be exactly correct. There is no way of satisfying those people who have made up their minds. Whatever proof they advance for their opinion is shattered; but they pluck victory out of the jaws of defeat, and in the disproof of their former argument they find a new one. One thing alone they reckon certain and necessary: Luke was an incapable and untrustworthy historian, and this must be demonstrated at all hazards and in any way that serves."

SIX

The Fourth Gospel

T HE THIRD AND FOURTH CHAPTERS of this book have
been devoted to a general discussion of the evidence
in support of the traditional authorship of St. Matthew,
St. Mark, St. Luke, and St. John. The special reasons for
accepting St. Luke as one of the greatest authorities on
the Roman Empire in the first century were discussed in
the last chapter.

The case for the Lucan authorship of the Third Gospel
has been incalculably strengthened by Ramsay's discoveries, but apart from this the arguments for the traditional
authorship of the Fourth Gospel are as strong as those for
the traditional authorship of the synoptic Gospels (so-
called because they agree in their general view of *synopsis*
of the events that they describe).

The determination with which the Fourth Gospel has been attacked is principally due to the difficulty of reconciling the traditional authorship with the denial of the deity of our Lord, and for this reason Unitarians, open or camouflaged, have been as eager as avowed atheists to discredit this Gospel. In point of fact, as we shall see, the proclamation of our Lord's deity is uncompromising in all four Gospels, and the Fourth Gospel presents no more exalted conception of our Lord's dignity than the synoptics. It is only because the *proportion* of such passages is greater in the Fourth Gospel than in the synoptics that a special effort has been made to prove that this Gospel was not written by a disciple of our Lord.

Skepticism about the Joannine authorship is not confined to Unitarians. A learned professor, who believed in the deity of our Lord, once remarked to me that he found it difficult to believe that a simple and unlearned Jew could have written a book that read like the work of an erudite D.D., and yet it is at least arguable that three years in the society of God is almost as good an education as three years at Oxford.

It is universally admitted, we have seen, that in the time of Irenaeus, the four Gospels were universally recognized in the Church as the work of the evangelists, to whom they are ascribed today, and we have seen that Irenaeus remembered the many occasions on which Polycarp repeated from memory what St. John and others had told him concerning our Lord. It is difficult to believe that either

Polycarp or Irenaeus could have failed to protest against the sudden appearance of a Gospel ascribed to St. John unless that Gospel had been ascribed to St. John from the date of its first publication to the Church. "If the Fourth Gospel be a forgery, it has had," as Salmon remarked, "the most wonderful success ever forgery had; at once received not only by the orthodox, but by the most discordant heretics— by Judaising Christians, Gnostics, Mystics—all of whom owned the necessity of reconciling their speculations with the sayings of this Gospel."

Eusebius has preserved for us a passage from Clement of Alexandria, born in the middle of the second century, in which Clement explains the special purpose with which the Fourth Gospel was written: "Last of all, John, perceiving that the bodily (or external) facts had been set forth in the other Gospels, at the instance of his disciples and with the inspiration of the Spirit composed a spiritual Gospel." It is therefore not surprising that St. John omitted much that the synoptics relate. There was no need to retell everything they had told. St. John's purpose was not to write a complete biography but rather to expound the doctrine of the Incarnation.

Now, though St. John nowhere contradicts the synoptic, there are many apparent discrepancies that are difficult to resolve, discrepancies that a forger, writing with the synoptics before him, would certainly have removed. It is a pure illusion to suppose that the second century was an uncritical age. The contempt with which the Fathers of that age spoke of the apocryphal Gospels is some indication of the difficulty that would have been encountered by a forger seeking to impose a spurious gospel on the Church. Dr. J.P. Arendzen in his valuable book *The Gospels, Fact, History or Legend?* gives many instances (pages 85-87) of the quickness of second-century Christians to detect and to denounce spurious writings. "When Bishop Serapion of Antioch," writes Dr. Arendzen, "on his visit in the parish of Rhossos found a Christian reading the so-called *Gospel of St. Peter*, it was not long before he fulminated against it. The Gnostic Acts of *John*, written about A.D. 106, were set aside and yet we are asked to believe that at the beginning of the same century a whole Christian community was taken in by a Gospel purporting to come from the son of Zebedee." The very fact that the Fourth Gospel was so different from the synoptics would have aggravated the difficulties of a forger in securing its recognition. From the first mention of the Fourth Gospel until 1792, when the Joannine authorship was questioned by Edward Evanson, an English deist, the only challenge to tradition came from an obscure and diminutive sect, the Alogi in the second century, who, according to Salmon, "consisted of Caius, and, as far as I can learn, of nobody else."

There is nothing in the Gospel that contradicts and there is very little that does not support the traditional view that the Gospel was written by St. John in extreme old age, toward the very end of the first century. It was, for instance, in the second century that the Sea of Galilee

82

came to be known as the Sea of Tiberias, and the way in which St. John introduces the name as ("the sea of Galilee, which is the Sea of Tiberias"—6:1) "would seem," writes Dr. Sanday, "to point exactly to the period of transition from the one form to the other."

If the Gospel had been written by a second-century Christian, we must credit the forger with an intimate knowledge, not only of the scenery of Palestine, but also of the outlook and prejudices of a Jewish contemporary of our Lord. Salmon has proved that the author possessed a detailed knowledge of the topography of Jerusalem and of Palestine and also of the local jealousies of first-century Palestine. The Galilean writer, resentful of the disdain with which the inhabitants of Jerusalem regarded his province, emerges in many passages: "Can anything good come out of Nazareth?" (1:46); "No prophet is to rise from Galilee" (7:52).

Further, the writer is familiar with the external aspect of the Temple, a heap of ruins in the second century, and also with its history. "The Jews then said, 'It has taken forty-six years to build this temple'" (John 2:20). According to Josephus, the building of the temple was begun about 20 or 19 B.C.; forty years from 19 B.C. brings us to A.D. 27, which is in full accord with the chronology of our Lord's life. The ancient world had little understanding of the science of chronology. To credit a second-century forger with such exact calculation for the sake of verisimilitude makes great demands on our credulity. There are many other passages that suggest that the author must have been a first-century Jew. The controversial questions that interest the author are those of the first century and not the second.

> The Messianic idea [writes Salmon] that pervades the Gospel is not that which prevailed after the Gnostic heresies arose, but that which existed before Jerusalem was destroyed, when the Jews still expected the Messiah to be a deliverer who should establish a temporal sovereignty and make the Jews the rulers of the surrounding nations. . . . St. John represents the prudent Jewish rulers as resolved to put down the prophesying of Jesus, because they feared that the political consequences of His assertion of His kingdom would be an unsuccessful revolt against foreign rule, the result of which would be that the Romans would come and take away their place and nation. . . . Remember that the state of Jewish feeling which I have described was quelled by the destruction of Jerusalem, and judge whether it is probable that a writer of the next century would have been able to throw himself into the midst of these hopes and feelings, and to reproduce them as if they were part of the atmosphere which he had himself breathed.

On the other hand, St. John reveals no knowledge of the controversies raised by the Gnostic heresies that broke out early in the second century.

Three times in the course of the Fourth Gospel, the author claims to write as an eyewitness, and again and again the writer seems especially concerned to record the reactions of the disciples to the events he describes. We have already noted the subtlety with which he describes the slow passage from agnosticism to unquestioning faith in the case of the man who was born blind. The author of the Fourth Gospel is no less concerned to describe a similar evolution in the case of the disciples (as, for instance, 2:17, 22; 12:16).

Many passages impress me with the conviction that I am reading the evidence of an eyewitness, as, for instance, the story of the woman taken in adultery, and the effect produced on St. John by the empty sepulcher, but perhaps the passage above all others, in which the accents of the disciple "whom Jesus loved" are most unmistakable, is the conclusion of the last chapter of the Fourth Gospel. Peter, to whom our Lord had foretold "by what death he was to glorify God," "turned and saw following them the disciple whom Jesus loved. . . . When Peter saw him, he said to Jesus, 'Lord, what about this man?' Jesus said to him, 'If it is my will that he remain until I come, what is that to you? Follow me!' The saying spread abroad among the brethren that this disciple was not to die" (John 21:19, 20-23).

There is something very appealing in this unconscious self-portrait of the aged disciple, still hoping against hope that his Lord would come again before he died and yet quietly correcting the expectation of his followers that our

85

Lord had promised that he would never see death. "But Jesus did not say," he is careful to add, "that he is not to die, but, 'If it is my will that he remain until I come, what is that to you?'"

We must indeed credit our hypothetical forger of the second century with consummate skill, if indeed this convincing picture is the invention of a later writer. Dr. James Drummond's book *Character and Authorship of the Fourth Gospel* (1905), which appeared shortly after the turn of the century, was all the more valuable as an index of the reaction in favor of the traditional authorship because Dr. Drummond's bias was certainly not in favor of tradition. One gets the impression that his concessions in favor of the trustworthiness of the Gospel are made without enthusiasm. Dr. Drummond draws attention to the fact that the author of the Fourth Gospel often "specifies particular days, for no apparent reason except that he remembered them, and sometimes even mentions the hour. He often names the disciple who was the speaker, even when the remark is not of consequence." Moreover, the writer frequently connects an incident with a particular place for no discoverable reason other than the fact itself. This precision of detail is admitted by William Wrede, a hostile critic and a convinced anti-miraculist, to be a "trump-card" in the hands of the defenders of the Gospel. Dr. Drummond is well aware that the only alternative to the belief that the Fourth Gospel was written by an eyewitness is the theory that it was written by a genius.

"It is sometimes said," he writes, "that to produce an untrue narrative possessing such verisimilitude as the Gospel,
would have been quite beyond the capacity of any writer of
the second century, such an author would be without example, such a work would be a literary miracle." So much Dr.
Drummond is prepared to concede, but he insures himself
against the peril of being classified with ordinary folk who
draw obvious conclusions from plain facts, by a caveat that
will no doubt mollify the anti-miraculists. "To assert," he
writes, "that an unexamined, unknown, and unmeasured
literary genius could not have done this or that appears
to me extremely hazardous." Nobody can be coerced into
preferring an extremely probable to a remotely possible
hypothesis, but surely it is "extremely hazardous" to reject
the obvious (even if *supported* by tradition!) in favor of the
improbable (even if *unsupported* by evidence).

There is nothing in the Fourth Gospel or in the literature of the first and second centuries to cast doubt on the
reiterated assertion of the writer that he was an eyewitness
of the events he describes. There is nothing in the literature
of the first two centuries to weaken our confidence in the
testimony of St. Irenaeus and in the unbroken tradition
of the Church in favor of the Joannine authorship of the
Fourth Gospel. There is no shred of evidence to support
the theory that the Fourth Gospel is "a literary miracle,"
the work of "an unknown and unmeasured literary genius."
The sole foundation for the desperate hypothesis is the
unscientific prejudice of the anti-miraculists.

The argument for an eyewitness authorship of the Fourth Gospel is little short of coercive, and under the pressure of evidence the anti-miraculists are in full retreat from the positions defended by Strauss and the earlier German rationalists. Adolf Deissmann, professor of theology at Berlin, like Adolf von Harnack, a Liberal Protestant with anti-miraculist leanings, stated in 1929 that he was convinced that the Fourth Gospel was "the work of a personal disciple of Jesus who later came under the predominant influence of the Pauline Christ-mysticism and Pauline-Christ cult."

In the last decade of the nineteenth century, Harnack, at one time a leader of the most radical school of biblical criticism, created a sensation by informing the astonished world of German scholarship in the famous preface to his *Chronologie der altchristlichen Literatur* that the oldest literature of the Church could be relied on for most of its details and that in the whole New Testament there was only one writing, the traditional authorship of which could be denied with confidence, the so-called second epistle of St. Peter. He summed up the result of the labors of twenty years (1876-1896) as constituting an unmistakable "return to tradition."

The recent discoveries, referred to in a previous chapter, and in particular the papyrus fragment of the Fourth Gospel dating back to the beginning of the second century, have, of course, accelerated this "return to tradition." But though the majority of modern anti-miraculists would be prepared to concede that the author of the Fourth Gospel was an eyewitness whose name was John, the unpleasantness of conceding so much to the traditionalists is mitigated by their refusal to admit that the author of the Fourth Gospel was John the son of Zebedee.

In an abridged quotation, which is to be found in a seventh-century epitome of the fifth-century history of Philip of Side, Papias refers to John and also in the same passage to John the elder. It is by no means clear whether Papias really means to speak of two Johns, or whether he has failed by slovenliness of composition to make it clear that he is merely naming John twice over, but this shadowy figure of Papias, John the Elder, has been credited with the authorship of the Fourth Gospel. We are bidden to believe that it was John the Elder who leaned on our Lord's bosom at the Last Supper and who is described in the Fourth Gospel as the beloved disciple.

The only fact in support of this theory is an alleged statement by Papias that both the sons of Zebedee were slain by the Jews, for which there is no independent evidence whatever and which is at variance with the unquestioned tradition of the early Christians that St. John had died a natural death.

The theory that the beloved disciple who leaned on our Lord's breast at the Last Supper was John the Elder involves, among other things, the supposition that there were thirteen disciples present at the Last Supper. Further, if the disciple "whom Jesus loved" (John 13:23) was not

89

John the apostle but John the Elder, there must have been in this little society a disciple who, though beloved beyond all others by our Lord, is not deemed worthy of mention by any of the synoptics.

And now comes yet a further difficulty. The name of the apostle John is never mentioned in St. John's Gospel, and whereas the synoptics, when they speak of John the Baptist, give him the title of Baptist to distinguish him from John the apostle, the Fourth Gospel speaks of him simply as John, for the one person in the Church who felt no necessity to distinguish between John the Baptist and John the apostle was John the apostle himself. No forger, as Salmon remarks, would have hit on such a quiet yet convincing mark of genuineness, but if the evangelist was *not* John the apostle, it is difficult to understand why John the apostle would never be mentioned. And if in our Lord's company there were two Johns, John the apostle and John "whom Jesus loved," it is still more difficult to understand why the only John mentioned by name in the Fourth Gospel should be John the Baptist.

The best that can be said for this hypothesis has been said by the late Canon Streeter, but he does not seem to meet the objections of Salmon or Sanday, much less the lucid and convincing argument developed by Dom Chapman in his book *John the Presbyter and the Fourth Gospel.* Shakespeare, as the humorist remarked, was written not by Shakespeare but by another man of the same name. I am reminded of this old jest by the writings of those who, in the words of Père Lagrange, O.P., "ont créé presque de rien un grand fantôme."[6]

The evidential value of the Fourth Gospel would be in no way impaired even if we were to concede that its author was John the Elder, for those who uphold this view believe that John the Elder was the "disciple whom Jesus loved," and therefore an eyewitness of the events he describes.

---

[6] "Have created a great phantom out of almost nothing.

SEVEN

The Claim

E T IN UNUM DOMINUM JESUM CHRISTUM, *Filium Dei unigenitum, et ex Patre natum ante omnia saecula. Deum de Deo; Lumen de Lumine; Deum verum de Deo vero; genitum non factum; consubstantialem Patri, per quem omnia facta sunt"* (Nicene Creed).

Christianity and divinity are words whose sharp edges have been blunted by the erosion of unbelief. A hundred years ago, men who accepted the first article of the Nicene Creed ("I believe in one God") but who denied the deity of our Lord described themselves correctly as Unitarians. Today many Unitarians claim the Christian name and profess to believe in the *divinity* of our Lord, a concession, the value of which is weakened by the fact that they also believe in their own divinity, for all good men, so we are told, have a spark of the divine. Divinity is a question of degree. God was more manifest in Jesus than in the greatest of the saints. The difference between Jesus and St. Francis of Assisi is a difference, not of kind, but of degree.

Historical Christianity, on the other hand, has always insisted that Jesus Christ is unique, differing from the saints, not only in degree but also in kind. To be a Christian, in any honest and intelligible sense of the word, is to believe that Jesus of Nazareth *claimed*, in the words of the Nicene Creed, to be "the only-begotten son of God, begotten of his Father before all worlds, God of God, Light of Light, true God of true God, begotten not made, being of one substance with the Father, by whom all things were made" and *proved* this claim by rising from the dead. The good word *divinity* is gone beyond recall. It has been annexed by Unitarians, avowed or camouflaged. Let us, therefore, substitute the word *Deity* or *Godhead* until such time as these words are, in turn, annexed and drained of all meaning by the Unitarians.

The special efforts that have been made to discredit the Fourth Gospel were inspired, as we have seen, by the fact that the Christology of St. John is particularly offensive to the Unitarian, open or disguised. But the difference between the Christology of St. John and of the synoptics is a difference of degree and not a difference of kind. There are far more passages in St. John than in any of the other Gospels of which the deity of our Lord is the theme, but the Godhead of Christ is as strongly, though not as frequently, asserted in the synoptics as in the Fourth Gospel. Whereas St. John and St. Paul were principally concerned to expound the implications of Christology, the synoptics addressed themselves to people who were less interested in theology than St. John, but who hungered for the human story of our Lord. It was their task to write the memoirs of Christ, leaving to others to develop the doctrine of Christ's person and nature. The epistles are, of course, earlier than the Fourth Gospel, and the Christology of the epistles is as explicit as the Christology of St. John. St. Paul, for instance, writes of the dear Son, who is "the image of the invisible God, the first-born of all creation; for in him all things were created, in heaven and on earth, visible and invisible, whether thrones or dominions or principalities or authorities—all things were created through him and for him. He is before all things, and in him all things hold together" (Col. 1:15-17).

Now, St. Luke must have been saturated with the christological doctrine of St. Paul, and yet St. Luke relates the story of the Crucifixion as a mere record of what happened, without attempting to develop, at least in that context, the Pauline interpretation of that unique event. Moreover, as the reader will see, the Christological texts that I am about to quote are drawn, not only from St. John, but also from the synoptics and the epistles. It would indeed be easy to prove that the apostles believed in the deity of our Lord without ever quoting from St. John. The apostles believed, not in the God-inspired prophet of the Unitarians, but in a Christ who, in the words of the Nicene Creed, "had been begotten of his Father before all worlds."

Before Abraham was, I am. (John 8:58)

You shall see the Son of Man ascending where he was before. (cf. John 6:62)

The glory which I had with thee before the world was made. (John 17:5)

He is before all things, and in him all things hold together. (Col. 1:17)

St. John and St. Paul proclaim that Christ is not merely inspired by God but the equal of God: "I in them and thou in me, that they may become perfectly one, so that the world may know that thou hast sent me and hast loved them even as thou hast loved me" (John 17:23).

St. Paul habitually couples the name of our Lord with the name of God on terms of equality.

Again, both St. John and St. Paul teach that it is only through Christ that we have access to the Father: "for through him we both have access in one Spirit to the Father" (Eph. 2:18). Those who still believe that the Christology of St. John is a second-century development should reread St. John and the Pauline epistles. It is impossible to deny the resemblance between the Pauline and Joannine Christology. If we turn from the Fourth Gospel to the synoptic, we find the same insistence on the deity of our Lord. It is not a human if God-inspired prophet who said: "Every one who acknowledges me before men, I also will acknowledge before my Father who is in heaven. . . .

He who receives you receives me, and he who receives me receives him who sent me." "And Jesus came and said to them, 'All authority in heaven and on earth has been given to me. . . . and lo, I am with you always, to the close of the age" (Matt. 10:32, 40; 28:18, 20).

St. Matthew represents our Lord as predicting that when the nations shall be summoned before the judgment seat of God, Christ will be seated on the throne of glory passing judgment on the human race. Moreover, judgment will be determined by our attitude to him: "As you did it to one of the least of these my brethren, you did it to me" (Matt. 25:40).

All the synoptics agree that Jesus was condemned for blasphemy by the high priest because he declared that he was the son of God (Matt. 26:65; Mark 14:62; Luke 22:69).

No rationalist has produced any plausible theory to explain *how* the belief in the deity of Christ originated. The contemporaries of Jesus were no readier to believe that some obscure carpenter was God than we should be. Had not Christ risen from the dead, the belief in his deity would have died with him. There is no escaping the dilemma that Christ was either God or a deluded madman intoxicated with a conceit overpowering in its absurdity. There is no trace in the words of our Lord of the humility that we associate with the saints. He never displays remorse, never suggests that he has fallen into sin, for the one text that is tolerant of some such suggestion is in reality an example of our Lord's gentle irony. Christ seldom stated his claims explicitly; it was his custom to elicit admissions of those claims by questions addressed to his disciples, and the questions that he poses in the words "Why dost thou call me good? None is good but God alone" admits of two answers: "You are neither God nor good," or "You are God, and therefore you are good."

The homage that is offered to Christ by those who reject his claims is irrational, for there is no justification for the scissors-and-paste interpretation of the Gospels that accepts as authentic those sayings of our Lord which commend themselves to the Modernist, or the Unitarian, but rejects his reiterated claims to be God. The texts that are exploited by anti-miraculists to justify the respect with which the overwhelming majority of non-Christians speak of our Lord are no more authoritative and have no better claims to be accepted as authentic than the texts that Strauss described as "an uninterrupted doxology only translated out of the second person into the first. . . . When an enthusiastic disciple puts utterances of his own pious enthusiasm into the mouth of Jesus, in the form of Jesus' utterances about himself, he does him a very perilous service." He does indeed—if Jesus was no more than man.

A minor argument for the deity of our Lord could be based on the reluctance of non-Christians to draw rational conclusions from their denial of our Lord's claims. Instead of condemning Christ as an impostor they seem spellbound by the ring of truth in every word that he uttered. No other founder of a religion has commanded an all-but-universal homage from those who deny his claims.

EIGHT

The Proof

E *T RESURREXIT TERTIA DIE secundum Scripturas"*
(Nicene Creed).

Every war produces a spate of books from people who explain how the war could have been averted if only their advice had been followed, and from generals who prove that the campaigns that they lost could in fact have been won, had they received the support they demanded. One is left with the vague impression that the world is divided into innocent men who write books and guilty men who don't.

Many years ago, two books were written by (and a third book was edited by) "guilty men" who made no attempt to conceal their guilt, who offered no defense for their sins and who never pleaded extenuating circumstances. One of these guilty men, called Matthew, described the weakness and the cowardice of himself and of the other apostles in the Garden of Gethsemane. Three times, he tells us, the apostles, whom our Lord had commanded to "watch and pray," fell asleep, and in the moment of his arrest they forsook him and fled. St. Mark, who wrote at the dictation of St. Peter confirms the account given by St. Matthew ("And he came and found them sleeping, and he said to Peter, 'Simon, are you asleep? Could you not watch one hour?'" [Mark 14:37]), and St. Mark, at St. Peter's dictation, records the great denial as a simple statement of unadorned fact. "But he began to invoke a curse on himself and to swear, 'I do not know this man of whom you speak.' And immediately the cock crowed a second time. And Peter remembered how Jesus had said to him, 'Before the cock crows twice, you will deny me three times.' And he broke down and wept" (Mark 14:71-72).

Because courage is the basic virtue, there is no weakness to which men are more reluctant to confess than cowardice. The story of those last scenes in the Garden of Gethsemane is not the kind of story that any of the actors would be in the least likely to invent.

"If evidence were needed," as Mr. Morison remarks in his notable work *Who Moved the Stone?*, "of the high standard of veracity prevailing in the Early Church, we have it here in its most convincing form."

In order to test the theory that the Gospels are works of fiction I recently reread Tolstoy's *War and Peace*, which many critics have described (in the words of one of them) as "the greatest novel ever written," but even those who consider that this book has been over-praised, and who would dissent from Turgeniev's later opinion that the best things in it are as good as anything that has been written, would find it equally difficult to accept Turgeniev's earlier verdict: "Nothing but comedy and charlatanism. There is no real development of character but simply the old method of transcribing hesitations, variation of the same emotions, or the same situations which he pitilessly puts into the mouth and conscience of each of his heroes." Though this is unjust, no character in this admitted masterpiece lives as Pontius Pilate lives, and this in spite of the fact that for every word St. Luke or St. John uses to describe Pilate, Tolstoy uses a hundred to describe Natasha or Pierre. Thirty years had passed since I first read *War and Peace*, and not one character or one episode remained in my mind, but could anybody who had ever read the trial scene forget the dream of Pilate's wife, or Pilate washing his hands before the people, or the final scene, which ends with the words: "What I have written, I have written" (John 19:22)?

Pilate, according to tradition, was born at Seville. He was a member of the *Ordo Equester* and served for a time under Germanicus. He laid the foundations of a successful career by marrying Claudia Procula, the granddaughter of Augustus Caesar, and it was probably to his connection with the ruling house that he owed his appointment as procurator of Judaea, and it may well be that but for his wife, he would have been recalled in disgrace before the Crucifixion. Pilate had little in common with the finer type of Roman proconsuls who tried to conciliate rather than to terrorize the subject peoples. He was stubborn, tactless, and vindictive when crossed.

Nothing, for instance, could have been more inept than his handling of the affair of the Ensigns. Knowing, as he must have done, that the Jews were fanatical in their determination not to admit graven images into Jerusalem, he yet insisted, for no discoverable reason, on sending Ensigns and Insignia of the Legions into Jerusalem, thereby provoking an insurrection that was quelled only when Pilate capitulated.

Before long he was in trouble again. To finance an aqueduct, he raided the "Corban," a fund devoted solely to religious purposes, and once again his actions provoked a sanguinary tumult.

The third incident was the affair of the votive shields that Pilate had installed in the Herodian Palace. He made no attempt either to understand or to discuss the Jewish objection to these tablets and yielded only when severely rebuked by Tiberius, to whom the chief men of the nation appealed. By this time Pilate must have realized that he had imperiled his career by these constant altercations with the Jews. He was in fact ultimately recalled in disgrace after the incident of the Samaritan imposture.

Reluctance to find himself yet again the storm center of a Jewish controversy may well have been one of the decisive factors in overcoming his determination to acquit Jesus. Of that determination there is no doubt. He turns desperately from one expedient to another . . . Herod . . . Barabbas . . . and he does not finally surrender until he hears the dreaded accusation "You are not Caesar's friend" (John 19:12). Pilate, in the pages of secular historians a tyrant, is transformed by the impact of Christ's personality into an irresolute and reluctant judge, his mind the battleground of conflicting influences; the fear of incurring Caesar's displeasure, the overpowering conviction that Jesus was both holy and innocent, and finally the influence of his wife. *"Have nothing to do with that righteous man, for I have suffered much over him today in a dream"* (Matt. 27:19).

It was, perhaps as Morison suggests, her influence that stiffened the Roman instinct for justice in Pilate, and while that influence lasted, his handling of the case was well-nigh perfect. "No juster hearing could any man have asked or obtained in any court of that far-off day. The restraining influence of one who clearly believed Jesus was innocent is obvious upon it," but in spite of all, he yields to the fanaticism of the Jewish camarilla. He surrenders, but at least he has the consolation of spoiling the Jewish triumph. In his own hand, he writes the inscription that is to be affixed to the Cross. "This is Jesus the King of the Jews" (Matt. 27:37). And that all who pass may understand what he has written, the inscription is written in Hebrew, in Latin, and in Greek. The Cross on which Jesus is to die shall proclaim Pilate's contempt for the Jews who demanded his death. They too shall be humiliated. "Here hangs *your* king," says Pilate in effect. Back stream the angry Jews, but Pilate has had enough. Pilate the irresolute disappears, and the stubborn procurator of secular history returns. He silences his Jews with words that men have quoted ever since to express unyielding finality. "What I have written, I have written."

It was not only Pilate's dormant conscience that awoke in Christ's presence. Into the lives of those whom he influenced, there entered a new awareness of beauty no less than of holiness. Simple peasants left all and followed him, and the loveliness of what they wrote endures forever. Beauty flowered in his footprints, and his presence sufficed to transmute the prose of common speech into poetry. The Pilate who is revealed to us in the pages of secular history was an insensitive tyrant whose practice was to solve the difficulties of his own creating by the bald prose of bloodshed and violence, but it was a very different Pilate who translated into the poetry of a sublime gesture an unavailing effort to transfer to others the responsibility for what he knew to be a tragic miscarriage of justice. "So when Pilate saw that he was gaining nothing, but rather that a riot was beginning, he took water and washed his hands before the crowd, saying, 'I am innocent of this righteous man's blood'" (Matt. 27:24). At the first examination of Jesus before the chief priests, the evidence of witnesses who had misunderstood one of our Lord's most perplexing predictions was an important part of the case against him. After

Jesus had driven the money-changers from the Temple, the indignant Jews asked him "what sign" he could show to justify this assumption of spiritual authority. "Jesus answered them, 'Destroy this temple, and in three days I will raise it up.' The Jews then said, 'It has taken forty-six years to build this temple, and will you raise it up in three days?' But he spoke," adds St. John, "of the temple of his body" (John 2:18-21). The witnesses at the trial can perhaps hardly be blamed for not understanding this, and both St. Mark and St. Matthew tell us that they testified that Jesus had claimed that he could destroy the Temple and rebuild it *within three days*. The witnesses contradicted each other, and on this charge the case for the prosecution failed.

The deeper significance of the phrase "within three days" and of Christ's cryptic allusions to the Temple did not, I think, escape the chief priests; for while the witnesses blundered and contradicted each other in their attempt, not necessarily dishonest, to represent Jesus as a madman who had asserted that he could destroy the Temple and rebuild it in three days, the chief priest seems to have suspected that what Jesus really meant was "If you kill me, I shall rise again in three days." And it is therefore easy to understand why they would have gone to Pilate "and said, 'Sir, we remember how that imposter said, while he was still alive, "After three days I will rise again." Therefore order the sepulchre to be made secure until the third day, lest his disciples go and steal him away, and tell the people, "He has risen from the dead," and the last fraud will be worse than the first.' Pilate said to them, 'You have a guard of soldiers; go, make it as secure as you can'" (Matt. 27:63-65).

Joseph of Arimathea, "a disciple of Jesus, but secretly for fear of the Jews," had obtained permission from Pilate to bury the body of Jesus and laid him "in a rock-hewn tomb, where no one had ever yet been laid" (John 19:38; Luke 23:53). A stone was rolled to the door of the sepulcher, and a guard was posted. St. John tells us that Joseph of Arimathea was assisted in the burial by that same Nicodemus who had come to our Lord by night.

Early on the following Sunday, a group of women made their way to the tomb in which Jesus had been buried. "It was widely accepted in the East," writes Morison, "that decomposition of a dead person set in on or about the third day after death. It was necessary, therefore, to perform the rites which the women had in view at the earliest possible moment consistent with the observance of the Sabbath. That moment was undoubtedly at sunrise on Sunday morning." The object with which these women visited the tomb was perfectly natural, and the hour at which they did so was consistent with their purpose.

The synoptics agree that Mary Magdalene was accompanied by Mary the Mother of James. St. Luke mentions the presence of Joanna, and St. Mark says Salome accompanied them. The argument from silence is often misleading, never more so than when exploited to prove that St. Matthew's account is inconsistent with St. Luke's because St. Luke mentions the presence of Joanna and St. Matthew does not. St. Mark tells us that on their way to the sepulcher, the holy women were preoccupied with the problem of the great stone placed before the door. "And they were saying to one another, 'Who will roll away the stone for us from the door of the tomb?'"

"And, behold," writes St. Matthew, "there was a great earthquake; for an angel of the Lord descended from heaven and came and rolled back the stone, and sat upon it. His appearance was like lightning, and his raiment white as snow. And for fear of him the guards trembled and became like dead men" (Mark 16:3; Matt. 28:2-4). And the women saw that the stone had been rolled back from the sepulcher, and going in they found not the body of Jesus.

Mary Magdalene was so overcome that she ran back to Jerusalem and told Simon Peter and John that they had "taken the Lord out of the tomb, and we do not know where they have laid him" (John 20:2), and while Mary Magdalene was on her way back to Jerusalem, two men in shining apparel (according to St. Luke) and the angel who rolled back the stone (according to St. Matthew), told the women who had remained in the sepulcher that Christ was risen: "Why seek you the living among the dead?" (Luke 24:5). And while this was happening, Peter and John were on their way to the sepulcher.

"There is one passage in particular," writes Salmon of the opening verses of the twentieth chapter of St. John, which by its graphic character forcibly impresses me with the conviction that I read the testimony of an eyewitness: I mean the account of the conduct of Peter and an unnamed disciple (who is unmistakably the Evangelist himself), when Mary Magdalene came running to tell them that the body of our Lord had been removed from the sepulchre; how the younger was foremost in the race, but contented himself with looking into the sepulchre; how Peter, with characteristic boldness, went in, and how the other disciple then followed the example set him. If any but an eyewitness devised all these details, so minute and so natural, we must credit him with a literary skill such as we nowhere else find employed in the manufacture of apocryphal Gospels. But there remains to be mentioned a touch so subtle, that I find it impossible to ascribe it to a forger's invention. Not a word is said as to the effect of what he had seen on the mind of Peter; but we are told that the other disciple "went in, and saw, and believed: for as yet they had not known the scripture, that Christ must rise again from the dead." Is it not plain that the writer is relating his own experience, and recalling how it was that the idea of the Resurrection opened on his mind as a reality? And lastly, note that we have here the work of no reckless forger. To such a one it would cost nothing to record that he and Peter had then seen our

Lord. But no; the disciples are merely said to have returned to their own home. It is Mary Magdalene who remains behind and first enjoys the sight of the risen Saviour.

St. Peter and St. John returned to their home. "But Mary stood weeping outside the tomb," and then suddenly she sees the two angels in white, who ask her why she weeps, and turning, she sees Jesus, whom she mistakes for the gardener: "Jesus said to her, 'Mary.' She turned and said to him in Hebrew, 'Rabboni!' (which means Teacher)" (John 20:11, 16).

If it could be proved that the various accounts that we possess of the events of the first Easter Sunday and of the subsequent appearances of Jesus to the disciples were not wholly consistent so far as details are concerned, this fact might be difficult to reconcile with any theory of direct inspiration or biblical inerrancy but would not invalidate the evidence so far as the central fact of the Resurrection is concerned.

"The usual characteristics of human testimony," writes Paley, "is substantial truth under circumstantial variety. That is what the daily experience of courts of justice teaches us." Thus, Clarendon tells us that the Marquis of Argyll was condemned and hanged on a Tuesday, but other historians assure us that he was condemned on the Saturday and beheaded, not hanged, on a Tuesday. Yet, in spite of the discrepancy on detail, nobody would deny that the execution took place. The evangelists did not profess to be writing complete biographies. They were writing memoirs, and the apparent discrepancies are, then, of no consequence so far as the thesis of this book is concerned, and I doubt whether even a fundamentalist would feel himself committed to a theory of biblical inerrancy that compelled him to believe not only that the evangelists accurately recorded the evidence of the witnesses to the Resurrection but also that those witnesses were themselves divinely protected from all error.

Consider the situation on the first Easter Sunday. Four women approaching the tomb in a mood of dejection, if not despair. They expect to find the sepulcher closed by a stone and protected by guards. Instead, they find the stone rolled back, the guards in a state of stupor, the tomb empty, and they are confronted by an angel (or by two angels) who announce the Resurrection. Despair gives place to joy, and the whole texture of life is suddenly and miraculously transformed. If the stories that the women told all agreed in the minutest detail, we would have to postulate a second miracle to account for so remarkable a concurrence. Be it noted that my thesis is not that the accounts cannot be reconciled, but only that such reconciliation in every detail would be contrary to all human experience. And it should be noted that a statement beginning, "Jones bore witness that . . ." may be accurate even if Jones's evidence is inaccurate, and therefore the inerrancy of Scripture is not disproved by an accurate record of what witnesses who were far from inerrant described. *Veritas citationis* is not the same thing as *veritas citati*. All of which is a digression, for we are not concerned in this book with theories of scriptural inspiration. It will be enough if we can show that the Gospels we have tested by the same criteria that we would apply to, say, other historical documents, attain to the standard of accuracy we associate with historical documents accepted as trustworthy by competent historians.

Of the four evangelists, St. John alone entered the empty tomb. The other evangelists had to rely on the reports of those who visited the sepulcher on that first Easter Sunday. The witnesses of those events and of the subsequent appearance of our Lord testified to what they themselves remembered, and it would be contrary to all experience if their recollections agreed down to the smallest detail. If, for instance, Joanna saw two angels, and Mary, in the language of the law courts, was prepared to swear to the presence of only one angel, there would be no necessary contradiction between the two accounts.

It seems to be improbable that any of the evangelists would have given an account that he knew to be inconsistent with the accounts of a predecessor without attempting to justify the correction of what he believed to be inaccurate in the earlier work. "The authentic text of St. Mark," writes Canon H.H. Streeter, "contains 661 verses. Matthew reproduced the substance of over 600 of these." St. Luke also made great use of the subject matter of St. Mark, but St. Luke never suggests that St. Mark's account is misleading in any detail. The argument is equally valid if we adopt Canon Streeter's view that St. Mark is older than St. Matthew or the traditional view that St. Matthew is older than St. Mark. St. John, who wrote with the synoptics before him, was writing for men to whom the main facts were known. His habit of trusting to the previous knowledge of his readers is responsible for some strange omissions, of which the most remarkable is the absence of any account of the Last Supper. This omission is the stranger because it is to the sixth chapter of St. John that we must turn for the first clear and definite exposition of the Eucharistic doctrine, "he who eats my flesh and drinks my blood has eternal life, and I will raise him up at the last day. For my flesh is food indeed, and my blood is drink indeed" (John 6:54-55). And yet St. John, who was the first to expound the Eucharistic doctrine, thought it unnecessary to repeat the description already given of the institution of the Eucharist at the Last Supper. No argument, therefore, can be based on the omission by any of the evangelists of incidents recorded by other evangelists.

St. John, who entered the empty tomb and who was an eyewitness of the appearances of the risen Lord would, we may be sure, have corrected anything in the synoptic Gospels that he knew to be false. The fact that neither St. John nor any of the other evangelists seems to be aware of discrepancies between their accounts and the accounts of their predecessors convinces me that if we knew what they knew, we would possess the key to the apparent inconsistencies in their narratives, and however puzzling some of these apparent discrepancies may be, "the substantial truth under circumstantial variety" to which all four evangelists bear witness is that Jesus was buried in the tomb of Arimathea and that the tomb was empty in the early hours of the first Easter Sunday.

NINE

The "Collective Hallucination" Hypothesis

T HE ANTI-MIRACULIST DOES NOT DENY that the disciples believed that they had seen the risen Lord, but
he asserts that they were victims of "collective hallucination." Anti-miraculists suffer from the collective illusion
that a polysyllabic phrase is a satisfactory substitute both
for proof and for explanation. The question at issue is (a)
whether it was the risen Lord whom the disciples saw or
(b) whether they merely imagined that they saw the risen
Lord.

To assert that they suffered from collective hallucination is merely to translate (b) into a polysyllabic phrase.

In his attitude to hallucinations the anti-miraculist is
unscientific. He postulates what is his business to prove.
He *assumes* that he can invoke the particular variety of

hallucination that suits his brief. The scientific historian, on the other hand, realizes that hallucinations have their own laws, and that it is his business to investigate those laws before postulating "collective hallucination" as a solution to the problem of the Resurrection.

We must not confuse hallucination with mal-observation. A clever conjurer can deceive his audience, and they may fail to observe things that only a keen-sighted and quick-witted person would detect, and the resultant hallucination is due to mal-observation. Abnormal people who are mentally unbalanced suffer from isolated illusions. Normal people under abnormal circumstances may suffer hallucinations.

Many years ago, Mr. Claud Elliot, now headmaster of Eton, and I, searched a Pyrenean peak on which a friend of ours had been killed. We had traveled all through the night from London and started on our search party within an hour or two of arriving at the little inn from which he started for his last climb. We were out of training and tired, and the strain of the search gradually began to tell. Every time we turned a corner, we expected to see our friend; again and again, we thought we saw his body stretched out on the rocks and heard the other members of the party shouting that they had found him. A vulture hovering near the cliff, as vultures will often hover for days before attacking a dead body, provided a macabre touch. These hallucinations were vivid while they lasted, but they never lasted for more than a second or two.

Monsignor Knox, in one of his sermons, quotes my experiences on the Pyrenean search party and adds:

> Isn't it possible, ask the critics of our religion, that the people who thought they saw our Lord after his Resurrection were in the same position as that?
>
> To which we answer, No. Whatever position they were in, they were not in the same position as that. Rather, they were exactly in the opposite position. A hallucination means seeing something else, and mistaking it for what you are looking for, as Arnold Lunn did in that Pyrenean peak; these people saw what they were looking for and, one and all, mistook it for something else. St. Mary Magdalene did want to find the Crucified, and it would have been natural enough if she had seen the gardener and mistaken him for our Lord. The curious thing is that she saw our Lord and mistook him for the gardener. The two disciples on the Emmaus road, who were thinking about our Lord and talking about him as they went, might have been pardoned if they had recognised his figure, wrongly, in that of some casual passer-by. But the fact is that they thought he was a casual passer-by when they really met him. The apostles in the Upper Room might easily have seen a ghost and taken it for their Master; but they didn't, they saw their Master and took him for a ghost. And again by the lake-side,

they might have been deceived by the accents of a strange voice, and thought it was his. It is more significant that they should have been deceived by the accents of his voice, and thought it was a strange one. They didn't run away with their first impressions, and tell unauthenticated stories of a miracle. They examined their first impressions and only by examination learned the miraculous truth.

And as Monsignor Knox remarked on another occasion, "Nobody is sure that he has found a half crown in his pocket as a man who puts his hand into a pocket expecting that it will contain a solitary copper."

Exhaustion, strain, and fear all played their part in creating those fleeting hallucinations on the Pyrenean peak, but no such background can be invoked to explain the appearances of our Lord to the disciples.

Nothing could be more natural than the setting in which Christ appeared to the disciples on their way to Emmaus. The story is told by St. Luke. Jesus joins them on their walk, just as any other pilgrim might. It was broad daylight, and the appearance of Jesus provokes none of that astonishment and perturbation we associate with the appearance of phantoms. And the stranger who joins them asks them why they are so depressed. "You must be a stranger in Jerusalem" is the reply, "or you could not have failed to hear the things that have happened these days." "What things?" asks the stranger; and the two disciples retell the sad story of their vanished hopes. "For, of course, we had hoped that it was he who was to deliver Israel."

Or again, read the story of doubting Thomas as told by St. John. No prejudice could be stronger than St. Thomas's. He insists on experimental proof before he believes and yields only to the irresistible pressure of stubborn fact. It is impossible to fit this story into the familiar pattern of hallucination.

Some Modernists maintain that the risen Christ was not a subjective illusion, but an objective vision. Read again your favorite ghost story, and then set it beside St. John's description of the appearance of the risen Lord on the sunlit shores of Tiberias. Every detail is as precise as the foreground of an Italian primitive: the charcoal fire on which the early morning meal was cooked, Simon Peter, impetuous as ever, leaping into the sea girt only in his fisherman's coat, and the net straining and yet not broken by the immense shoal of fish. And finally nothing could be more quietly convincing than St. John's record of the words that the risen Lord spoke beside the shores of the lake, the prediction that Peter would be martyred, the hint that perhaps St. John might tarry till he came. That this last chapter should be pure fiction is, at least, an arguable hypothesis, but it is impossible to explain St. John's story of what happened and what was said on this occasion by the hypothesis of "collective hallucination." In all the records of alienists, there is no instance of a "collective hallucination" remotely resembling this. It is indeed ironic that those who cannot accept the Resurrection because it is unique are driven to postulate something no less unique, a "collective hallucination" of a type not paralleled in all the records of human illusion, an illusion that has had an infinitely greater effect on the course of history than any admitted fact.

"If you say," writes St. Thomas Aquinas, "that no one has seen a miracle performed, I will reply this: 'It is agreed that the whole world worshipped idols, and persecuted the faith of Christ, so the histories of the pagans record. But all were converted to Christ, wise, noble, rich, powerful and great men at the preaching of simple men, who were both poor and few. This was either done miraculously or not. If it was done miraculously, my point is proved. If it was not, I say that there could not be a greater miracle than that all the world should have been converted without miracles'" (*De Symbolo Apostolico*).

No serious critic denies that St. Paul wrote the first epistle to the Corinthians, in which he records the principal appearances of the risen Lord to the disciples. It is therefore impossible to maintain as an alternative to the theory of "collective hallucination" the hypothesis that the story of these appearances is a second-century myth. That the disciples believed that they had seen the risen Lord is admitted by atheists, agnostics, Unitarians, Jews, and Modernists.

Our problem is to account for the origin of a belief so contrary, not only to human experience, but also to their own expectations, for the disciples hoped for an earthly triumph and refused to believe that Jesus would be rejected by his own people. And because they did not wish to believe in the Cross, they found no room in their minds for the Resurrection, which, like the Cross, had been foretold.

Very significant in this context is the conversation of two disciples with the risen Christ, whom they had failed to recognize on the walk to Emmaus. They told him how the chief priests and our rulers handed Christ over to be sentenced to death. "But we had hoped that he was the one to redeem Israel. Yes, and besides all this, it is now the third day since this happened" (Luke 24:21). And they describe with no apparent conviction, the finding of the empty tomb by the women and also by some of the apostles "but him they did not see," and it is clear that these disciples at least were unpersuaded by the fact that the women reported "that they had even seen a vision of angels, who said that he was alive" (Luke 24:23, 24). It was not until they returned to Jerusalem that the disciples who walked to Emmaus learned that "the Lord had appeared to Simon" (cf. Luke 24:34).

The reluctance to accept the evidence of women is a convincing touch, for if the story had been *invented*, we may be very sure that the discovery of the empty tomb would not have been attributed to *women*. "The mind of the first century about women," writes Mr. H.P.V. Nunn in his valuable book *What Is Modernism?*, "even in Christian circles is clearly seen in the Epistles and in the First

Gospel where we are told that the disciples marvelled that our Lord even spoke to a woman. . . . If the story is true, no further explanation of the important part played in it by women is needed. It is only another proof of the honesty of the witnesses of the Resurrection who admitted the slowness and lack of faith of the Apostles and the ready faith of the women." Mr. Nunn quotes, very appositely in this connection, St. Augustine's "Thou hast given power to men to form an idea about themselves from others and to believe many things about themselves on the authority, *even of feeble women."*

It was no sudden hallucination that converted the disciples, but stubborn fact that prevailed against stubborn doubts. It was not only Thomas who doubted. "And seeing him," writes St. Matthew of the appearance on the Mount of Galilee, "they worshiped him; but some doubted" (Matt. 28:17). Even after the Resurrection, the disciples were still so far from understanding the message of the Cross that they asked him, "Lord, will you at this time restore the kingdom to Israel?" (Acts 1:6), for they were still dominated by the Jewish belief that the approval of God was shown by the prosperity of the righteous and his disapproval by misfortune and death.

"I have been young," exclaimed the Psalmist, "and now am old; yet I have not seen the righteous forsaken or his children begging bread. But transgressors shall be altogether destroyed; the posterity of the wicked shall be cut off" (Ps. 37:25, 38).

It was not until St. John entered the tomb and found it empty "and the napkin, which had been on his head, not lying with the linen cloths but rolled up in a place by itself. Then the other disciple, who reached the tomb first, also went in, and he saw and believed; for as yet they did not know the scripture, that he must rise from the dead" (John 20:7-9).

It was difficult for the disciples to believe in the Resurrection because this belief conflicted with all human experience. It was difficult to believe in Christ because loyalty to Christ involved a breach with the church of their fathers. We are tempted to forget that the disciples were Jews, for the influence of Christian art is so strong that we tend to think of them as Nordic or Latin Christians and not as Asiatic Jews. Religion is never more powerful than when it is closely associated with the national loyalties of an oppressed race, as, for instance, in Palestine under the Romans, or in Serbia during the Turkish occupation, or in Ireland during the long Anglo-Protestant ascendancy. It was as difficult for the disciples to break away from the Synagogue as it would have been for Irish peasants during the penal times to apostatize from the Catholic Church.

It is inconceivable that a mere hallucination could have provoked and maintained this spiritual dislocation of their lives, a dislocation that involved a complete breach with their past. Sooner or later, the remonstrances of those who loved them and the bitter reproaches of those who despised them as apostate would have eroded their faith in the objective reality of what they believed that they had seen. As the opposition increased and as the possibility of martyrdom became more and more apparent, their confidence in the hallucination would inevitably have weakened.

Moreover, no hallucinations are identical, and inevitably as the memory of the phantoms faded, the disciples would have begun to compare their own memories of what they believed that they had seen, and the inevitable discrepancies would have reinforced their growing doubts. Finally, these men had to stand the supreme test of martyrdom, and they were not of the stuff of which martyrs are made, for they abandoned Jesus and fled at the moment of his arrest and Peter subsequently denied him.

It is very hard for a man to eradicate even small failings, for character is stubborn in its resistance to change. The disciples were average men, neither heroes nor cowards, but subject—as ordinary men are subject—to collapse under great strain, and it is difficult to believe that a mere hallucination could have transformed these men, who panicked in Gethsemane, into the dynamic apostles who were not only ready to break with their church, their relations, and their friends, but who also proved themselves undaunted by flogging, imprisonment, and the ever present prospect of martyrdom. Nothing but a certitude, rocklike in quality, could have produced this amazing transformation. Morison writes:

Somehow the rugged fishermen, Peter and his brother Andrew, the characteristically doubting Thomas, the seasoned and not too sensitive tax-gatherer, Matthew, the rather dull Philip, intensely loyal but a little slow of apprehension, do not fit easily into the conditions required for an absolutely unshakable collective hallucination. And if it is not both collective and unshakable it is of no use to us. The terrors and the persecutions which these men ultimately had to face, and did face unflinchingly, do not admit of a half-hearted adhesion secretly honeycombed with doubt. The belief has to be unconditional and of adamantine strength to satisfy the conditions. Sooner or later, too, if the belief was to spread it had to bite its way into the corporate consciousness by convincing argument and attempted proof.

So potent was the influence of this alleged hallucination that the disciples, whose nerve had failed in Gethsemane, returned to Jerusalem prepared to measure themselves against the brilliant and unscrupulous camarilla that had already crucified their Master. If the anti-miraculist hypothesis is sound, this was a hopeless venture, a last desperate flicker of the fanaticism that should have died with their Master on the Cross. *And yet they won.* This heterogeneous collection of Galilean peasants not only provoked a schism in their own church but, within twenty years, had left their mark in every town from Caesarea to Troas of the Mediterranean littoral and, within fifty years, had begun to disturb the peace of the Roman Empire.

It is easy to take the past for granted and thus to discount the overwhelming obstacles that Christianity had to overcome before it could hope to make the faintest impression on the sophisticated world of Roman Society and Roman Letters. "Jesus has not been ignored," writes Professor Adolf Deissmann, "by pagan authors. He is also mentioned by the old Jewish texts"—and also, as we shall see, by the great Jewish historian Josephus. But it was not until Christianity began to disturb the Roman peace that allusions to this troublesome sect begin to appear in Roman literature, as, for instance, in the works of Tacitus, Suetonius, and Pliny. "Christianity," writes Deissmann, "was a religious movement among the lower classes, at first a small hidden mustard seed. The men of literature and the whole aristocracy, had they noticed it in the period of its beginnings, would not have mentioned it, regarding it as a despicable, proletarian movement. Thus, the fact that even later on, early Christianity was only seldom mentioned by pagan authors is simply due to its social structure. The Gospels are not quoted in the Graeco-Roman literature just because these thin modest little books are never found on the bookstalls of the great capitals, but like a kind of secret literature, they were hidden in the houses of those unknown people who, with a few exceptions, composed the Christian brotherhoods." The Roman intelligentsia was as uninterested in this obscure criminal, executed by a Roman procurator, as the Victorians would have been in some Sudanese fanatic executed by the sentence of a British court martial.

If we translate the triumph of the disciples into modern terms, we have to imagine the worship of some obscure Mahdi replacing the worship of Christ in St. Paul's Cathedral. "We cannot insist," as Morison so justly remarks, "on the strict reign of causality in the physical world, and deny it in the psychological. The phenomenon which here confronts us is one of the biggest dislodgements of events in the world's history, and it can only be accounted for by an initial impact of colossal drive and power. . . . Does this rather heterogeneous body of simple folk, reeling under the shock of the Crucifixion, the utter degradation and death of their leader, look like the driving force we require?"

TEN

The Empty Tomb

EVEN IF COLLECTIVE HALLUCINATION could be invoked to explain the belief of the disciples that they had seen the risen Lord, the skeptic would still have to account for the empty tomb. The fact that the tomb was empty was not denied by the enemies of Christianity when the disciples first began to preach the Resurrection. The Pharisees made no attempt to prove that the body of Jesus had not been buried in the tomb that the women visited on Easter Sunday, or that the body of Jesus was still in the tomb in which he had been buried.

"It is impossible," writes Morison,

to read the records of the period without being profoundly impressed by the way in which, for friend and foe alike, the tomb of Jesus sinks into utter and undisturbed oblivion. . . . No one pretending to have an intimate and special knowledge seems to have said: "not here was he ultimately buried, but there." Instead of these quite natural consequences flowing from so extraordinary an event, we get this stony appearance of indifference. From the moment that the women return from the Garden the tomb of Jesus passes, historically, into complete oblivion. . . . The assumption that the tomb was empty seems to have been universal. The only controversy of which we have any record, and it was clearly a heated one, was on the vexed question as to whether the disciples had secretly removed the body.

The tomb was infinitely important because it was completely ignored. Had the tomb been a center of interest and controversy, the task of the Christian apologist would have been much more difficult. Had the body of Jesus never left the tomb, the Pharisees would have thrown the tomb open for inspection and invited the dupes of this new heresy to see for themselves the body of Jesus, still lying where he had been buried. Had the disciples believed that the risen Lord was a phantom, permitted to return to earth, the tomb in which his body still lay would have become a shrine for those pilgrims who believed in a spiritual resurrection of their Master, but not in the physical Resurrection of his body.

The forgotten tomb was remembered only when the tomb had passed into history.

The disciples could have given no clearer proof of their own serene unquestioning certitude than their readiness to preach the Resurrection in Jerusalem itself within a few hundred yards of the tomb, from which the body could be produced to refute them if their faith was vain. Strauss admits that this fact is embarrassing: "We leave the body in the tomb . . . a place well known and easy to find, and then if the disciples had taken upon themselves to preach the Resurrection of Jesus in the same town less than forty hours after his burial, can one believe that the Jews would not have run to the tomb, brought out the body, and confuted such an outrageous statement by a public examination of it? Or, rather, how could the disciples have been able to believe in the Resurrection when they had only to look into the tomb which was quite close at hand, to convince them that it had never taken place?"

Strauss's attempt to meet this difficulty will be discussed in due course.

Seven weeks after the Resurrection, a Galilean fisherman collected a crowd in Jerusalem and began to tell them about the Resurrection, and on that very day, the day of Pentecost, St. Peter baptized three thousand converts. A staggering achievement, and yet . . . we are not staggered. Because it is so natural for us to be Christian, we forget how unnatural it was for the Jewish contemporaries of St.

Peter to accept his belief in the Resurrection of a Galilean peasant whose execution had been a nine-day wonder in Jerusalem. All analogies are imperfect, none more than those that seek to transpose the events of our Lord's life into a modern or a quasi-modern setting, but it is not unprofitable to search for a parallel, not to the Christ in whom we believe, but to the Jesus of Loisy and Strauss, the futile victim of his own delusions.

Let us suppose that a peasant in eighteenth-century Ireland had persuaded himself and a few friends that he was a reincarnation of Jesus and had been excommunicated by his bishop and subsequently hanged in Dublin as a rebel by the British, and that within fifty days of his death, one of his followers had proclaimed on St. Stephen's Green that the executed rebel had risen from the dead, and converted three thousand Dublin Catholics to this new heresy on the day on which it was first preached. Suppositions such as these are no more inherently improbable than the story that Luke, of whose accuracy as a historian we have given proof, recounts in the second chapter of Acts. And, of course, in this hypothetical case, the production of the body of the executed rebel by the British authorities would have demolished the pretensions of the new sect.

Though anti-miraculists are unhampered by any sense of obligation to produce evidence in support of their alternatives to the Resurrection, no anti-miraculist has affirmed that the Pharisees did, in point of fact, produce the body of Jesus. On the contrary, their ingenuity is concentrated on the attempt to explain why the Pharisees were unable to confront the apostles with the dead body of the man whose Resurrection they were preaching.

Let us consider the various hypotheses that have been put forward by the anti-miraculists.

1. *Jesus did not die on the cross, but recovered in the tomb, from which he subsequently escaped.* We are asked to assume that Jesus could have escaped from a tomb that was closely guarded. But if we accept the implied theory that the story of the guards is a Christian invention, we have still to explain the *ultimate* disappearance of his body. If he rejoined the disciples and died surrounded by his followers, his tomb would have been known and venerated as a shrine. If, on the other hand, he left them once again and vanished completely from their ken, some hint of the confusion and perplexity that this unexplained disappearance must have caused would have found its way into Christian literature. And, finally it is, as Strauss himself insists, "impossible to believe that a man who had crept, half-dead, out of the grave, weak and ill, needing medical attention, bandaging and indulgence, and who must finally have yielded to his sufferings, could have produced on the mind of his disciples the impression that he had triumphed over death and the grave, the Prince of Life, and yet it was this impression which was the basis of their future ministry. Such a resuscitation could only have weakened the

impression which he made on them in life and in death, and could not possibly have transformed their sorrow into enthusiasm, or their reverence into worship."

2. *The women made a mistake and went to the wrong tomb.* This is the kind of theory that could be advanced only by learned men who are more familiar with texts than with human beings. People with less learning but more sense will not need to be told that if the belief in the Resurrection began when the women visited the wrong tomb, it would have ended when the Pharisees invited all concerned to inspect the body of Jesus in the right tomb.

3. *The sepulcher in which Jesus was first buried was never intended to be a permanent tomb. Joseph of Arimathea removed the body and transferred it to another sepulcher.* No adequate motive has been suggested for a proceeding on behalf of which no evidence has ever been produced. Joseph was a man of principle, "a respected member of the council," so St. Mark describes him, "who was also himself looking for the kingdom of God" (cf. Mark 15:43). If Joseph had moved the body of Jesus to another tomb, he must have known that St. Peter was the victim of an illusion when he asserted that the body of Jesus "had not seen corruption" (cf. Acts 13:37). Joseph, according to St. Matthew and St. John, was a secret disciple of our Lord. He followed him because he loved truth, and we may be sure that he would not have allowed the disciples of the Master whom he revered to base their teaching on a lie.

Under the influence of his gentle correction, the Resurrection would have been preached in the form in which it is often preached today, as a spiritual resurrection, and the appearances of our Lord explained as a vision of a phantom and not as the objective appearance of the actual body that Joseph had buried in the tomb.

It should also be noted that Joseph must have been assisted in his task by two or three servants. Why should these servants have maintained silence when they could have refuted by a word the birth of a new religion that they knew to be based on an illusion? No explanation has been suggested to account for the conspiracy of silence into which Joseph and his servants must have entered, if this hypothesis is accepted.

4. *"It is quite possible,"* writes Strauss, *"that it [the body] was thrown into some dishonourable place with those of other executed criminals, and in this case his disciples may have, at first, had no opportunity of seeing the body. Later, when they preached the Resurrection, even their opponents would have found it difficult to recognize his body and to provide proofs of its identity."* Of the controversy which this theory postulates, about the identity of a corpse exhumed from a common grave, there is no hint in the records and literature or traditions of the period.

Note, once again, the recurring contrast between the Christian who offers proof in support of his claims, and the anti-miraculist who offers none. *Quod gratis affirmatur, gratis negatur.* That which is without argument affirmed can be denied without argument, but if argument is needed to demolish this fantasy, such argument is not difficult to provide.

Loisy, who adopts this hypothesis, attempts to render it more plausible by the statement that the body of Jesus was not at the disposal of the disciples. Loisy, who would, perhaps, have been less highly praised for his scholarship, had his scholarship been enlisted on behalf of orthodoxy, here betrays his ignorance of Roman law, under which Pilate was compelled to hand over the body of Jesus to whoever demanded it. To admit that the disciples gave way to a fit of panic in Gethsemane does not compel us to concede that they were consistently base and cowardly. Had this been the case, they would have deserted Jesus when he first began to attract the hostility of the Pharisees. It is difficult to believe that they would have allowed their beloved Master's body to be thrown into an *unehrlichen Orte* (dishonorable place) without making the least attempt to give it that decent burial which the laws of Rome permitted. "The weakest and least esteemed of Christians of a later age," writes Mr. Nunn, "would never have allowed such a thing to happen to the bodies of their martyred friends, as the genuine martyrologies and the catacombs bear witness." But the final and the conclusive refutation of this hypothesis is the fact that if the body of Jesus had been buried in a common pit, the Pharisees would, at least, have made an effort to exhume it to refute the Resurrection.

5. *The disciples stole the body from the tomb.* This was the hypothesis advanced by the Pharisees, and *therefore* should take priority, for reasons to be explained, of all hypotheses put forward by modern skeptics. If the disciples had stolen the body of Jesus, they would have known that he had died the death of a deluded fanatic and that he had not risen from the dead. Why should the disciples conspire to impose upon the world a new religion that they knew to be false? A spontaneous falsehood, as Origen pointed out, could not have nerved the disciples to announce with such unflinching courage a doctrine that was so perilous in its probable consequences. What occult compensation could have nerved them to break with their church and their friends and to accept martyrdom in the propagation of what they themselves knew to be a monstrous and superfluous lie? "I readily believe," wrote Pascal, "those witnesses who get their throats cut."

Let us try to reconstruct the situation as it must have seemed to the council of chief priests and elders who were summoned to consider the perilous situation that was created by the preaching of the Resurrection on the day of Pentecost. Three thousand Jews had joined the schism. If three thousand Irish Catholics apostatized in Dublin within a few days, the effect on the Irish hierarchy would be no more devastating than the impression produced on the Pharisees by the rise of this new religion.

Their first problem was to account for the empty tomb, for the one fact that was not in dispute was the fact that the body of Jesus was no longer in the tomb in which it had been laid. Even their worst enemies have never accused the Jews of stupidity. The council of priests and elders was, in some sense, an intellectual elite. The Sanhedrin were not only skillful dialecticians but were also practical politicians. Nobody can read the account of the trials of Jesus before the high priest and before Pilate without admiring the skill with which this very weak case was pressed to a successful conclusion. The witnesses might contradict each other, and Pilate might be more than reluctant to convict, but the prisoner of whose innocence he was convinced was crucified at his command.

The forensic genius that was exploited to secure the condemnation of Jesus must have been invoked to explain away the Resurrection. The tomb was empty, and inevitably every explanation, save the true one, must have been considered in the attempt to find a plausible alternative to the Resurrection.

It is obvious that the contemporary explanation of the empty tomb advanced by those who had every interest in refuting the Resurrection is far more worthy of our consideration than explanations advanced many centuries later by men whose hypothesis cannot be tested as the hypothesis of the Sanhedrin could be tested by the cross-examination of contemporary witnesses. *To put it more simply, the Sanhedrin knew what they could get away with.*

Benjamin Jowett was once asked for a definition of tragedy. He replied, "A beautiful hypothesis killed by a fact."

There may have been many such tragedies as the Sanhedrin passed in review a succession of beautiful hypotheses to explain the empty tomb, hypotheses, all of which were killed by facts, of which the Sanhedrin were aware but of which Renan, Strauss, Loisy, Rashdall, and Major are no longer aware. I find it difficult to believe that no member of that keen-witted group was alert enough to hit upon the various explanations of the empty tomb that have since been put forward by Renan, Strauss, Loisy, Rashdall, and Major. And it seems to me probable that the hypothesis they eventually adopted, the theory that the disciples had stolen the body, though far from satisfactory was indeed the best that could be advanced by men who hoped to convince their contemporaries, conversant with the relevant facts of the contemporary scene, and therefore less easily misled than the readers of *The Freethinker* or *The Modern Churchman*.

But there is at least one fact which suggests that some of the Pharisees were not particularly impressed by their own hypothesis. When St. Peter was summoned before the council and refused to cease preaching Christ, many of the council wished to put him to death, but Gamaliel, "a teacher of the law, held in honor by all the people," warned them, "'If this plan or this undertaking is of men, it will fail; but if it is of God, you will not be able to overthrow them. You might even be found opposing God!' So they took his advice" (Acts 5:34, 38-40). They would probably not have consented had they been wholly convinced by

their assertion that the disciples had stolen the body of
Jesus and were therefore preaching something they knew
to be false.

Had the Pharisees been able to suggest an explanation
of the empty tomb that quieted all reasonable doubts, it is
inconceivable that this explanation would not have been
recorded by the great Jewish historian Josephus. Josephus
was born within ten years of the Crucifixion. He was a
member of a distinguished priestly family and attached
himself to the party of the Pharisees at the age of nine-
teen. When the Jewish revolt broke out in the year 66,
Josephus was chosen by the Sanhedrin at Jerusalem to
be commander-in-chief in Galilee. He was captured after
the fall of the fortress of Jotapata and was a witness of the
destruction of Jerusalem and the Temple.

Josephus had associated from his youth with distinguished scholars. He possessed to a pre-eminent degree the
intellectual curiosity of a great historian. It is inconceivable that so great a historian with such peculiarly intimate
relations with the priestly nobility should have been left
in ignorance of any satisfactory explanation of the empty
tomb, if such explanation in point of fact existed. And yet
here is what he actually wrote about the Jesus whose claims
he was prepared neither to accept nor to deny:

> About this time lived Jesus, a man full of wisdom,
> if one may call him a man. For he was the doer of
> incredible things, and the teacher of such as gladly

accepted the truth. He thus attracted to himself many Jews and many of the Gentiles. He was the Christ. On the accusation of the leading men of our people, Pilate condemned him to death upon the cross. Nevertheless, those who had previously loved him, still remained faithful to him. For on the third day he again appeared to them living, just as, in addition to a thousand other wonderful things, prophets sent by God had foretold. And at the present day the race of those who call themselves Christians after him has not ceased. *(Jewish Antiquities*, chap. 18).

The genuineness of this passage has been attacked, but no criticism has met the objection that this passage occurs in *all* the codices and manuscripts of Josephus's work. It is asking a great deal of the reader to expect him to believe that *all* the codices and manuscripts were tinkered with by Christians, and that in every case the same *identical* interpolation was surreptitiously introduced into the original text.

The tendency of modern critics is to accept the genuineness of this famous passage. Harnack regards this as proved almost beyond doubt, and critics who do not err on the side of conservatism support this view, notably Prof. Burkitt, Prof. Emery Barnes *(Contemporary Review,* January 1913), Louis Gray, the distinguished coeditor of the *Encyclopedia of Religion and Ethics,* and among continental critics, Bretschneider, Böhmert, Langen, Daubuz, Kneller, and others.

Furthermore, my contention that Josephus would have recorded any plausible explanation of the empty tomb put forward by the Sanhedrin still holds, even if one accepts the reconstruction of the passage which H. St. John Thackeray attempts in his *Josephus the Man and the Historian* (pp. 125-153). This authority on Josephus, who formerly held that the whole passage was a Christian interpolation, finally accepted as genuine a nucleus sufficiently long to prove my point.

Our next witness is St. Justin Martyr, who was converted to Christianity about A.D. 130 in his thirtieth year. Among his works is the record of a disputation in the city of Ephesus with Tryphon, one of the most celebrated Israelites of the day. Justin discusses in great detail the principal arguments whereby contemporary Jews sought to refute and to discredit Christianity, and the dialogue is of great interest for the light it throws on the early evolution of Christian apologetics. And it is clear from this dialogue that the Jews of the second century still repeated and made their own the explanation of the empty tomb, which St. Matthew attributes to the chief priests. "You have sent," says Tryphon, "chosen and ordained men throughout all the world to proclaim that a godless and lawless heresy has sprung from one Jesus, a Galilean deceiver, whom we crucified, but his disciples stole him by night from the tomb, where he was laid when unfastened from the cross, and now deceive men by asserting that he has risen from the dead and ascended to heaven."

Toward the end of the second century, Celsus published his famous attack on Christianity. The intimate and exact knowledge that he displays of Jewish history and Jewish thought compels us to believe that he would have been aware of the strongest arguments against the Resurrection current among the Jews, but, he too, insists that the disciples had stolen the body.

It would be contrary to all experience if the defense of orthodoxy against a great schism—and in the eyes of the Jews, Christianity was a schism—had left no trace in the written records and traditions of the parent church. We know exactly how the contemporary apologists for the Catholic Church replied to the Greek schismatics of the ninth century and to the Lutherans and Calvinists of the sixteenth century. It is inconceivable that an effective contemporary refutation of the Resurrection could have vanished without trace from Jewish history and tradition.

Dr. Samuel Krauss, the author of the article on Jesus in the *Jewish Encyclopedia*, has his own explanation of the Resurrection, but the only *contemporary* explanation to which he alludes is the charge that the disciples stole the body. It is not until the beginning of the third century that we find the first hint of an alternative explanation in the terrible passage of *De Spectaculis 30*, in which Tertullian rejoices at the prospect of beholding the torments of those who persecuted the Christians. "This is he," exclaims

Tertullian to the Jews, "whom you bought from Judas. This is he whom the disciples stole away in secret, that it might be said that he had risen"—so far there is no breach with tradition, but Tertullian hints, with bitter irony, at an even more absurd explanation when he adds "unless it was the gardener who removed the body, for fear that his lettuces should be trampled down by the crowd of visitors."

The gardener as the *deus ex machina* to disprove the *deus ex sepultura* reappears in that strange byproduct of irrational hatred *Toledot Yeshu*, a medieval "life" of Jesus by a Jew. According to *Toledot*, the disciples sought for the body and, being unable to find it, used the disappearance of the body as proof that he who had been crucified had ascended into heaven. And they reported this to Queen Helena. It then appeared that Judas the gardener had removed the body from the grave and used it as a dam to keep the water out of the garden and had flooded the tomb. Then there was joy in Israel. The body was taken before the queen at Jerusalem, and the Christians were shamed.

This grotesque story is significant. It proves that from the first the Jews had been forced to admit that the tomb was *empty* and had been compelled by the controversial significance of the empty tomb to seek for some explanation other than that put forward by the Christians.

ELEVEN

The Testimony of St. Paul

E VEN IF ALL THE GOSPELS had vanished, we could still prove that the first Christians were convinced that they had seen the risen Lord and that it was this belief that transformed the disciples into the dynamic apostles of the new revelation of God through Christ.

"All critics," writes the distinguished Jewish scholar C.G. Montefiore, "now believe that the first Epistle to the Corinthians was really written by St. Paul and that chapter fifteen is, therefore, the oldest extant tradition about the Resurrection."

Even Ferdinand Baur, most radical of critics, who reduced the number of genuine epistles to four, the *Hauptbriefe*, as he called them, included among these four the two epistles to the Corinthians.

In the fifteenth chapter of the first of these epistles, St. Paul affirms "that Christ died for our sins in accordance with the scriptures, that he was buried, that he was raised on the third day in accordance with the scriptures, and that he appeared to Cephas, then to the twelve. Then he appeared to more than five hundred brethren at one time, most of whom are still alive, though some have fallen asleep. Then he appeared to James, then to all the apostles. Last of all, as to one untimely born, he appeared also to me" (1 Cor. 15:3-8).

Saul, who was born in Tarsus, the son of a Roman citizen, and whose other name was Paul, was formed by two great traditions. He belonged by birth to a family with a hereditary connection with the Jewish church, and he was educated in an atmosphere of deep piety and strict observance of his religious obligations. On the other hand, he was influenced by the Graeco-Roman culture, and there is evidence of wide reading in some of his speeches. He seems to have been familiar with the works of Aratus, Menander, and Epimenides.

In the first phase of the Jewish-Christian controversy, Saul of Tarsus was the outstanding figure on the side of the Pharisees, and this for many reasons. He was a man with whom one instinctively associates the big word *genius*. Even the bitterest opponents of Christianity have never denied his greatness. On the contrary, there is a tendency to exaggerate his achievement and to give him credit for founding the Christian church. Dr. Krauss, for instance, describes him as the real founder of Christianity in the *Jewish Encyclopedia.*

St. Paul was a superb advocate. He adjusted his appeal instinctively to the mood and temper and beliefs of the different audiences he addressed—the Greeks, for instance, on the Areopagus, or Felix or, again, Agrippa. He was a master of the art of dividing the opposition, as, for instance, in his speech before the council, recorded in Acts 23. How subtly he contrived to drive a wedge between the Pharisees who did and the Sadducees who did not believe in a future life!

When he entered the Jew-Christian controversy, as a partisan of the priests, he must inevitably have exploited to the full his forensic genius in a desperate attempt to discover a satisfactory solution to the problem of the empty tomb, and the fanatic hatred with which he persecuted the Christians was inevitable once he had accepted the theory that it was the disciples who had stolen the body. This upright and profoundly religious man had an immense reverence for the truth. Even the author of the article on St. Paul in the *Jewish Encyclopedia*, who does not find it easy to write with sympathy of one whom he regards as the greatest of apostates from Judaism, concedes that he was "a mighty battler for truth." It is easy to appreciate the loathing with which Saul of Tarsus must have regarded this heretical sect whose leaders were deliberately attempting to impose upon their fellow countrymen a new religion that they knew to be fraudulent.

The serenity with which Stephen went to his death may well have shaken him. Men do not die for what they know to be false, but Stephen's death produced no immediate weakening in Saul's determination to destroy Christianity. On the contrary, he was on his way to organize a further persecution in Damascus when his life was revolutionized by an experience that anti-miraculists have tried in vain to explain away.

If the vision on the Damascus road was a hallucination, it was one of those hallucinations that seem peculiar to the New Testament record, a hallucination that was revolutionary in its radical transformation of character and outlook. We know something of the effect of ordinary hallucinations, the gradual weakening of character, and the disintegration of mind, but as we read the letters of St. Paul's middle and later life, we find, as Morison rightly says, no trace of any weakening,

> rather the coming to maturity of a fine intellect, an intensely logical and ordered mind. . . . When Saul was really convinced that he had seen the risen Jesus, the immense and overpowering significance of the empty tomb swept for the first time into his mind. It was as though the great stone itself had crashed away his last defences. He saw that if the disciples were not deceivers, they then were *right*— right through the whole range and gamut of their claim. He realized why you could not associate a

148

martyrdom so glorious as that of Stephen with a vulgar deception involving connivance with the abduction of a corpse. He began to understand why Peter was so sure, and why everyone connected with this strange movement was so unaccountably joyous and so immovably convinced.

)

TWELVE

Christianity Without Miracles

L IBERAL PROTESTANTS, CATHOLIC MODERNISTS, and Anglican modernists with negligible exceptions believe in the possibility of dissociating Christianity from the belief in miracles. The typical Modernist either formally rejects miracles or at best regards them as wholly irrelevant to the Christian faith. Modernists object to miracles for a variety of reasons—the less well-informed because they assume that science has disproved miracles, the better informed because they maintain that though miracles are theoretically possible, they are unworthy of their Creator. It is, they feel, beneath the dignity of God to work miracles. Most Modernists would heartily endorse C.E.M. Joad's contemptuous reference to miracles in our published correspondence *Is Christianity True?* After paying the conventional tribute to the beauty of Christ's teaching, he rebuked me for "wasting time over vulgar marvels" such as the Resurrection.

If Jesus was nothing more than an inspired prophet, clearly no miracles were needed to recommend his teaching to the world, and it is easy to understand why those who, in effect, deny the deity of our Lord find it easy to dispense with miracles. Camouflaged Unitarians are usually ready to concede "divinity" to Jesus, a handsome concession, the value of which is discounted, as I have already remarked, by the fact that they are equally ready to claim divinity for themselves. In this respect, if only in this respect, most Modernists would agree with Mrs. St. Clair Stobart, who writes: "If Jesus was Divine by virtue of being Spirit, has not every man and woman for whom spirithood is claimed, equally the right, according to our showing, to be called Divine? And is not then the differentiation between the divineness of Man and the divineness of Jesus again one only of degree?"

No, a thousand times no. Historical Christianity has always insisted that Jesus Christ was unique, differing from all other men not only in degree but also in kind. And because Jesus Christ was unique, his entry into and his departure from this world were also unique.

Even non-Christians are influenced by the habit of the Christian centuries, and acquiesce without surprise to the fact that some of us still believe that he who filled the heavens with flaming stars was born in a manger and

152

played with other little boys in the streets of Nazareth. It is not surprising that men should boggle at this tremendous claim, but it is plain foolish to pretend that it is more difficult to believe that Jesus rose from the dead than that the son of a Jewish carpenter was the creator and the sustainer of the universe. The very reverse is the case. Spiritualists who accept the miracles but who deny the Godhead of Jesus are more logical than those who pretend to accept his divinity and yet repudiate the unique corroboration he provided for a unique claim.

The holiness of his life and the beauty of his teaching would not have persuaded any of his contemporaries that he was God, and of our contemporaries there are none who would be prepared for one moment to consider his claims to be divine, had not millions of Christians accepted those claims because of their miraculous endorsement.

The early Christians accepted Christ as a divine teacher because they believed in his miracles. Some of his sayings can be paralleled in rabbinical and even in classical literature. Plato, for instance, had urged men to repay evil with good, but it was left to the Christian saints to practice what Plato preached. The modern secularist, the product in some ways of a Christian tradition, often writes as if the paradoxes of Christ are nothing more than the truisms of progressively minded humanitarians. But why should we love our enemies? A Roman would have dismissed the suggestion with contemptuous laughter. An occasional philosopher might preach such sentiments, but the world had to wait until Christ had risen from the dead before these sterile moralizings could be transformed into action. In every age, there have been thousands of Christians who have patterned their lives on Christ. How many have patterned their lives on Plato? Men have married poverty, laughed in the flames, and jested on the rack, not only because they were impressed by the moral beauty of the parables, but also because they believed in the miracles that the Modernist rejects. Modernists admit that Christianity would not have survived the Crucifixion, had not the disciples been subsequently convinced that Jesus had risen from the dead, and yet they are naive enough to believe that Christianity could continue to survive after repudiating a belief that they concede to have been indispensable to the primitive Church.

Modernism is a parasite that draws such vitality as it possesses from the dogmas that it denies. It is only because all Catholics and the great majority of Anglicans and Free Churchmen still believe in the Resurrection that there are still pulpits from which a non-miraculist Christianity can be preached.

The belief in the Godhead of our Lord and the belief in the Resurrection stand and fall together. Those who repudiate the Resurrection have set their feet on a road that leads from Christianity to Unitarianism, open or camouflaged. It is therefore not surprising that Modernists who revere Jesus as a mystic, and nothing more, should feel that miracles are a superfluous and even distasteful element in the Gospel story. And it may be that this violent prejudice against miracles is, in some cases, inspired by the unconscious realization that the acceptance of miracles implies the acceptance of the Godhead of our Lord.

Three assumptions are implicit in the apologetics of Modernism:

- Assumption A. *The Modernist welcomes but the traditionalist distrusts the discoveries of modern science.* Modern scientific research has gone some way to establish the reality of many of those psychical phenomena that Modernists have always attributed to fraud or mal-observation, and the late Dr. Alexis Carrel is not the only famous scientist whose investigations of the miracles at Lourdes have led to conclusions highly distressing to the Modernist (see chapter 2).

Neither Joad nor Haldane, in our published controversies, could reply to my challenge to name an established scientific fact that was inconsistent with the dogmas of the Church.

The case, then, stands thus. The discoveries of modern science, insofar as they have any bearing on the question, have *weakened* the anti-miraculist case and are therefore welcomed by the traditionalist.

Nothing, of course, could be *less* scientific than the Modernist approach to the problem of miracles, for David Strauss defined, once and for all, the guiding principle that all true Modernists accept, the great dogma that "in the works and person of Jesus there was nothing supernatural allowed to remain." For the Modernist, as for Strauss, this negative dogma is essential, but there is nothing in the least scientific in deductions based on an unproved dogma.

It is not with science that the Modernist establishes his concordat but with the pseudoscience popular with all those who are eager to exclude the Creator from all influence on his creation.

There is, I shall show in a later chapter, an odd parallel between the controversial methods of the Modernists and the mechanistic-evolutionists.

• Assumption B. *The Modernist welcomes but the traditionalist distrusts the results of modern scholarship and biblical criticism.* It is not, as we have seen, the traditionalist but the Modernist who is embarrassed by modern discoveries, such as those of Ramsay in Asia Minor or the Rylands fragment of St. John, assigned by paleographers to the beginning of the second century.

• Assumption C. *Intellectual integrity is the distinguishing note of Modernist scholars. Unconscious dishonesty is only too common in the apologetics of the traditionalists.* Few apologists, religious or political, as the case may be, are wholly successful in resisting the temptation to overstate their own case and to misrepresent their opponent's case, but the temptation is more difficult to resist in the case of Modernism for the good reason that the unadorned facts point to the traditional conclusion. Modernists, incapable of conscious dishonesty, sometimes stoop to very questionable methods in their attempt to avoid orthodox conclusions. I have a great admiration for Dr. Inge. He has the courage to defy the fashion of the moment and has often defended unpopular causes. He is a master of English prose and is the author of four devotional addresses published under the title *Speculum Animae* which no Christian—Catholic, Protestant, or Modernist—could read without profit, but his attempt to prove that our Lord anticipated Dr. Inge's dislike of miracles is disingenuous rather than convincing.

"A dramatic vindication," writes Dr. Inge, "of God's omnipotence in the world of phenomena was precisely what the contemporaries of Christ desired to see and it was precisely what He did *not* come to earth to provide. A wicked and adulterous generation seeketh after a sign. Verily I say unto you, there shall no sign be given unto this generation." And at this point, Dr. Inge breaks off the quotation from St. Matthew (12:39). St. Matthew continues with a reference to the miracle of Jonah and a prediction of the miracle of the Resurrection: "except the sign of the prophet Jonah. For as Jonah was three days and three nights in the belly of the whale, so will the Son of man be three days and three nights in the heart of the earth" (Matt. 12:39-40).

Thus, the words that Dr. Inge omits from his truncated quotation flatly contradict the forced interpretation that he deduces from the words he quotes.

The truncated quotation enjoys a considerable vogue in Modernist circles. At the end of a lecture I gave in Oxford, the late Canon B.H. Streeter quoted the same text that Dr. Inge had quoted in support of the same conclusion and stopped short at the same point. Now, Canon Streeter was a distinguished New Testament scholar, and yet he seemed genuinely surprised when I completed the truncated quotation.

The twelfth chapter of St. Matthew, from which Dr. Inge quotes to prove that our Lord refused to work miracles, contains the account of two miracles, an allusion to a third miracle, and a prediction of the Resurrection.

It has been suggested that Dr. Inge was confusing two texts, Matthew 12:39 and Mark 8:12. The words "wicked and adulterous" occur in St. Matthew and in Dr. Inge's quotation, but not in St. Mark, who also omits the reference to Jonah.

Mark 8 opens with the story of the miraculous feeding of the four thousand (verses 1-9); reports our Lord's rebuke to the disciples, in the course of which he reminds them of the feeding, on two different occasions, of the four thousand and the five thousand (verses 14-21); reports the miraculous healing of a blind man (verses 22-26) and our Lord's prediction of his Resurrection (verse 31). No fewer than twenty-three verses out of thirty-eight have to be removed before this chapter could receive the *nihil obstat* of Dr. Inge, twenty-three verses, all of which describe or allude to miracles. Is it reasonable to expect us to believe that St. Mark, who records or describes in one chapter no fewer than *four* miracles, meant to imply that our Lord disapproved of miracles? Whatever else verse 12 of this chapter ("no sign shall be given to this generation") means, it cannot mean *that*.

The Modernist pretention to monopolize "modern scholarship" and "scientific criticism" is nothing but an audacious camouflage for the neo-Lutheran rule of faith, for there is nothing scientific about a scissors-and-paste criterion that assumes the inerrancy of all texts that accord with Modernist presuppositions and rejects as interpolations all those that do not. Christianity, we are assured, can dispense with miracles because the beauty of his moral teaching proves Christ to be divine. But our authority for his teaching is no greater than our authority for his miracles. *For what shall it profit a man, if he shall gain the whole world and lose his soul?* I do wish some Modernist would explain by what intelligible canon of criticism he can accept as a historical record these words that will be found in verse 36 of Mark 8 and reject as spurious the twenty three verses of the same chapter in which four miracles are described or discussed.

The late Dr. James Moffatt was a distinguished New Testament scholar, some of whose works I have read with enjoyment and, I hope, with profit, but his famous translation of the New Testament is marred by mistranslations where prejudice has triumphed over scholarship. Like other Modernists, he prefers to talk of the *divinity* rather than the Godhead of our Lord, and he accordingly translated the first verse of St. John: *The Logos was divine*. Now, there is a perfectly good Greek word for *divine—theios—* but it happens that the word St. John used was *theos*, which means "God," and the correct rendering of the first verse is *not* "The Logos was divine" but "The Word was God."

Similarly, "Take; this is my body" is a correct translation of Mark 14:22, whereas Dr. Moffatt's "Take this, it means my body" is a glaring example of the subordination of scholarship to sectarian prejudice. No Modernist has written with greater eloquence on the contrast between his own rectitude and the dishonesty of Roman Catholic traditionists than Dr. Coulton. I have compared Dr. Coulton's standards with those of the writers whom he has pilloried, but I am well aware that the examples I have selected from the writings of eminent Modernists could easily be paralleled in the writings of the traditionalists. All I am concerned to prove is that there is no justification for assumption C, the contrast between the alleged intellectual integrity of Modernists and the alleged dishonesty of their opponents.

Modernists do not seem to be aware of the characteristics that must be ascribed to God, if Modernism is true. Modernists admit that Christianity would never have survived had not the apostles believed in the Resurrection, and few, if any, Modernists would disagree with the Rev. H.D.A. Major's statement that "they who look into the face of Jesus Christ see in Him the very essence of the Creator's moral and spiritual nature."

If, then, Christ did *not* rise from the dead, and if the noblest of religions originated in a myth, it would seem that God permitted "the very essence of His moral and spiritual nature" to be revealed through a religion based on deception. "Will you speak falsely for God, and speak deceitfully for him?" said Job (Job 13:7), but man, it would seem, had need of a lie which God permitted, the false statement that Jesus rose from the dead. But those who believe that God is the God of truth will not easily believe that God would commend his revelation to mankind by means of a deception. And yet this would seem to be the view of the late C.G. Montefiore, a Liberal Jew whose attitude to Christianity is not easily distinguishable from that of many Modernists. In his famous book *The Synoptic Gospels* (pages 399 and 404), he writes:

> It is hard to believe that great religious results should have had not quite satisfactory causes. The subjective vision was, in one sense, an "illusion." Yet upon that illusion hinged the great religious result which we call Christianity.
>
> J. Weiss has most ably shown the historical sequence of the Resurrection stories. First come the visions. These we must assume actually took place. Not that Weiss believes in any objective reality behind them. They were what we should now call hallucinations, though as he urges, the modern Christian believer, who also believes in God's rule

161

in history, may justly hold that these hallucinations were the will of God.

An even greater difficulty is to reconcile Modernism with the Christian egalitarianism, which finds room not only for the rich and the poor but also for the learned and the unlearned. Traditional Christianity is a universal religion that appeals to all races and to all classes, to the duke no less than to the crossing-sweeper, to the European and to the African, to the genius and to the washerwoman, but to whom does Modernism appeal? To a very limited cross section of Western and North American civilization. Like Roman Stoicism, which in many ways it resembles, Modernism presupposes a reasonable income and a good education. Modernism is over-represented in academic circles and unknown in the slums. Modernists send no missionaries and would make no converts if they did. Modernism is the fad of the few and can never be the religion of the many. Its noblest literature seems to me to be open to much the same criticism as that which St. Augustine passed on the writings of the Platonists. "In these pages there is no trace of the face of compassion, the tears of penitence . . . a broken and a contrite heart. No man in these writings hears the voice of one who called, 'Come unto me, all ye who labour.'" *Nemo ibi audit vocantem: Venite ad me, qui laboratis.* I doubt if the destitute and despairing would receive much comfort from the gospel of Bishop Barnes: "*an empirically reached theism will ultimately maintain itself as the most reasonable explanation of man and his world,"* and I would hesitate to console a soldier dying on the battlefield with Bishop Barnes's handsome compliment to Christ's ethics, which, he tells us, *"give an edge to theism. Such ethics create the pacifist, ready at the cost of his own life to preach peace between the nations."*

Dr. Major, an unconquerable optimist, expects that Modernism will make the Christian religion universal and provide the Church with an apologetic that will win the English people to Christ. Now, whether Modernism is true is a question of opinion, but whether Modernism attracts the modern man is a question of fact, which can be settled by the simple and well-tried scientific method of counting noses. Dr. Major has only to make a tour of churches next Sunday to discover that modern men are not filling the churches in which timeless truths are re-interpreted to adjust them to the latest fad, disguised as "modern thought." Whatever else modern man may want, it is clear that he does not want Modernism.

Unitarianism, avowed or disguised, has no survival value. Presbyterianism, which seemed in a fair way to capture Cromwell's England, died out in the eighteenth century because it could not resist the Unitarian infiltration. English Presbyterianism was re-imported from Scotland in the nineteenth century.

Every great religious revival in the English-speaking world has been based on a re-emphasis on the deity of

Christ and the Resurrection. Methodism in the eighteenth century and the Oxford Movement of the nineteenth century represented a reaction against anti-miraculist tendencies. Continental Protestantism is moribund because Continental Protestantism has succumbed to the prophets of "Christianity without miracles." I have often asked my Swiss friends whether they could name a single *young* man who was a regular attendant at a Lutheran or Zwinglian or Calvinistic place of worship. The type is certainly unknown among the young Swiss whom I have met among the mountains or on the snows, but from time to time, so a Swiss once told me, a simple man will hire and fill a hall by preaching the old evangelical gospel of the Christ who died upon the Cross for our sins and rose again on the third day. No man who preaches that message with conviction need ever despair of a congregation.

THIRTEEN

"Miracles" Without Christianity

I CONCEDE," SAID MY FRIEND, "that the evidence for the Resurrection is impressive, but you won't convert me to Christianity by proving that Jesus rose from the dead, any more than you would convert me to spiritualism by coercive evidence in support of spiritualistic miracles. Jesus may have worked miracles, but the evidence for his miracles is no stronger than for David Hume's, and nobody pretends that David Hume was divine. Jesus may have been an exceptionally powerful medium, a super-Hume, if you like, but if you want to persuade people that he was divine you've got to produce something more impressive than psychical phenomena."

In my youth it was fashionable to assert that the possibility of miracles had been disproved by science; today it is increasingly fashionable to maintain that miracles are so common that they prove nothing.

The materialism that appealed to science is moribund, and there are signs which suggest that whereas materialism was the principal rival to Christianity in the nineteenth century, spiritism is destined to prove the chief heresy of the twentieth century.

Spiritism is the correct term for those who believe that it is possible to communicate with the spirits of the departed, and it is unfortunate in the interests of exact thought that spiritists should have been allowed to annex the word *spiritualism*, for all those who reject materialism are spiritualists. Spiritism is a formidable rival to Christianity because the spiritist, unlike the secularist or Modernist, does at least make an honest attempt to apply the scientific method to the greatest of all problems. He is unhampered in his search for truth by the negative dogma that "miracles do not happen." His approach is inductive rather than deductive. He begins with particular facts before proceeding to general conclusions. His theory does not fit all the facts and is inconsistent with many of the facts, but it explains far more facts than the theories of the secularists, Liberal Protestants, and Modernists. There are, as I know, many Christians who are so repelled by the apologetics, literature, and consequences of spiritism that they are impatient of all attempts to examine dispassionately the residuum of supernormal phenomena that are not explicable by fraud or hallucination or mal-observation, but the Christian rationalist must not follow the example of "rationalists" and pseudoscientists. He must practice what T.H. Huxley preached.

"Science," wrote Huxley to Charles Kingsley, "seems to me to teach in the highest and strongest manner the great truth which is embodied in the Christian conception of entire surrender to the will of God. Sit down before fact as a little child, be prepared to give up every preconceived notion, follow humbly wherever and to whatever abysses Nature leads, or you shall learn nothing. I have only begun to learn content and peace of mind since I have resolved at all risks to do this."

"At all risks." We shall see. Huxley's reactions to unwelcome hypothesis were as unscientific as those of a fundamentalist to fossils. His resolve to "sit down before fact" did not survive the invitation he received to examine the mediumship of Daniel Dunglas Home.

Daniel Home, the subject of a recent book, was perhaps the most remarkable medium who ever lived. He was never exposed as fraudulent, and he never accepted a fee for seances. "A highly desirable characteristic of Home's mediumship," wrote that distinguished scientist Lord Rayleigh, "was the unusual opportunity allowed to the sense of sight." Home always objected to darkness at his seances. Home became famous as a medium in the 1850s, and a committee was appointed by the Dialectical Society of London to investigate the phenomena alleged to occur in his presence. Thirty-four members of standing were appointed, most of whom agreed to serve in the belief that they would be instrumental in unmasking a fraud. The committee met on forty occasions, and the report they presented caused such dismay that the Dialectical Society declined to publish it, whereupon the committee published it at their own expense. Here are some extracts from the report:

> Thirteen witnesses state that they have seen heavy bodies—in some instances men—rise slowly in the air and remain there for some time without visible or tangible support. Five witnesses state that they have seen red-hot coals applied to the hands or heads of several persons without producing pain or scorching. . . . In presenting their Report your Committee, taking into consideration the high character and great intelligence of many of the witnesses to the more extraordinary facts, the extent to which their testimony is supported by the reports of subcommittees, and the absence of any proof of imposture or delusion as regards a large portion of the phenomena . . . deem it incumbent upon them to state their conviction that the subject is worthy of more serious attention and careful investigation than it has hitherto received.

Huxley was invited to join this committee. He declined. "Supposing the phenomena to be genuine they do not interest me. The only good that I can see in the demonstration of 'Spiritualism' is to furnish an additional argument against suicide. Better live a crossing-sweeper than die and be made to talk twaddle by a 'medium' hired at a guinea an hour."

"*Supposing the phenomena to be genuine—they do not interest me.*" What a lamentable confession for a scientist! Huxley failed to distinguish between the phenomena and the spiritist explanation of the phenomena. Thirteen witnesses of "high character and great intelligence" had stated that they had witnessed the phenomenon of levitation. Now levitation, if it occurs, necessarily involves a revolutionary restatement of orthodox dynamics, and, as such, should arouse the interest of scientists. The committee that Huxley was invited to join believed that there was a prima facie case for levitation and were entitled to expect the cooperation of scientists in the investigation of this strange phenomenon. Admittedly Huxley would have been entitled to decline the invitation on the ground of pressure of work, but his petulant reply was a clear indication that he considered that the proposed investigation did not deserve the serious consideration of any respectable scientist. The spiritist would have been entitled to reply: "Sit down before fact like a little child, be prepared to give up every preconceived notion, follow humbly wherever and to whatever abysses Nature leads, even to the abyss of a spiritist paradise, or you shall learn nothing."

It was left to scientists such as Sir William Crookes, Sir Oliver Lodge, William Barrett, Charles Richet, Cesare

Lombroso, Albert von Schrenk-Notzing, and others to investigate these phenomena. There are fashions in science as in other things, and in science, as elsewhere, it is dangerous to defy fashion. Sir Oliver Lodge told me that he had lost the presidency of the Royal Society because of his spiritualistic views, and I have already quoted Alexis Carrel's statement that he began his study of Lourdes miracles in 1902 "at a time when the documents were scarce, when it was difficult for a young doctor, and dangerous for his future career, to become interested in such a subject."

In the long history of the Church, there is only one case, Galileo's, in which a scientist has been persecuted by theologians because of his scientific views, but many scientific pioneers have suffered from the persecution of their colleagues. In the nineteenth century, scientists defied at their peril the materialistic philosophy that was dominant in the world of science. A scientist might be a Christian in his private life, but he incurred the suspicion of heresy if he challenged mechanistic evolution or investigated the supernormal phenomena of the seance room or the miracles at Lourdes.

"The tyranny of the Zeitgeist," wrote Thomas Dwight, Parkman Professor of Anatomy at Harvard, "in the matter of evolution is overwhelming to a degree of which outsiders have no idea; not only does it influence (as I must admit that it does in my own case) our manners of thinking, but there is oppression as in the days of the 'terror.' How very few of the leaders of science dare tell the truth concerning their own state of mind! How many feel themselves forced in public to do a lip service to a cult they do not believe in!"

The contrast between the nineteenth and twentieth centuries to which Sir William Ramsay drew attention in the sphere of New Testament criticism is even more marked in the sphere of psychical research. Psychical research has become respectable and an increasing proportion of professional scientists are prepared to concede the genuineness of certain supernormal phenomena.

An unbiased investigator who reads *Experiences in Spiritualism by D.D. Home,* by the Earl of Dunraven, must accept one of two alternatives. Either supernormal phenomena occurred or one must fall back upon complete skepticism as to the possibility of certifying facts by human testimony. The book opens with an impressive list of fifty witnesses, men and women of responsible position, who were present at these seances and who (with four exceptions who were inaccessible) testified to the accuracy of these reports. Of this book, Lord Rayleigh, at one time president of the Royal Society, writes, "I find it difficult to accept what one may call the 'knave and fool theory' of these occurrences, but failing that it would seem to follow that one must accept the possibility of much that contrasts strongly with ordinary experience."

Many psychical phenomena depend on a mysterious substance, "ectoplasm." The medium goes into a trance; a cloudy, filmy substance emerges from the body of the medium and slowly organizes itself into the shape of a hand, or foot, or face, or—in rare cases—of a complete human body. Ectoplasm has been studied under rigid test conditions by scientific investigators. It has been photographed, weighed, and cinematographed. The French government subsidized the Institut Métapsychique in Paris as an institution of "public utility," and it was at this institute that the paraffin glove test was first attempted. Dr. Gustave Geley and Professor Richet, who never abandoned his materialistic philosophy, prepared a paraffin bath. The "spirit," a complete materialzation of a human body which moved and responded to commands, was requested to immerse his hand into the paraffin, with the result that the "spirit" hand emerged covered with a thin fragile coating of paraffin, a fragile shell about a sixteenth of an inch in thickness. A human being could not withdraw his hand from such a delicate paraffin shell without breaking it; for the hand could not pass through the narrow opening where the shell had solidified near the wrist. The "spirit," however, dematerialized its hand in the paraffin shell, which was therefore left intact.

The paraffin shells were preserved and made permanent by filling them with plaster. The lines on the hands and fingerprints were proved to be completely distinct from those on the hands either of the medium or of the sitters. In order to prove that the paraffin shells were not manufactured outside and introduced surreptitiously into the seance room, Dr. Geley mixed cholesterin with the paraffin and proved that the paraffin gloves produced during the seance contained cholesterin.

Scores of these "gloves" have now been produced at seances, but the attempts of scientists and conjurors to reproduce them have failed. Houdini spent some weeks at Notre Dame University attempting to reproduce paraffin gloves. I was shown the result.

Whereas in many of the paraffin gloves, the hands are closed, the thumbs bent and the fingertips joined to the palm, and in some cases two clasped hands are shown, in Houdini's experiment, the fingers were extended and close together and Houdini had managed to extract his extended hand without breaking the shell, but even so, the contrast between the swollen distorted shells that he produced and the delicate paraffin shells of the seance, perfect in their molding and showing all the lines of the hand, was most striking. Moreover, Houdini worked under his own conditions, whereas the medium produced these shells under conditions dictated by Richet.

The truth is that conjurors have completely failed to reproduce the more striking psychical phenomena under the rigid test conditions imposed on mediums.

The reality of telepathy and clairvoyance would seem to have been established by the experiments at Duke University, carried out by Dr. J.B. Rhine, associate professor of psychology. These are fully described in *Extra-Sensory Perception* (Faber and Faber), to which Professor William McDougall, F.R.S., the distinguished psychologist, contributes an introduction. For the purpose of these experiments, packs of cards were used, which contained cards of five different types, marked respectively with a circle, a square, a cross, an asterisk, and two wavy lines. There were equal numbers of each of these five cards in all the packs that were used. If I am asked to guess the cards as they are turned up in another room and to call them out as they are turned up, I shall expect, there being cards of five different types, to be right once in 5 times (20 percent). If I scored 10 hits (40 percent) out of the first 25 attempts, I would not be particularly surprised, but if I scored 40 percent, instead of 20 percent, out of the first 100 trials, I would begin to wonder whether I did not possess some telepathic faculty, for the probability of doubling the proportion of hits that one has a right to expect under the laws of chance rapidly decreases with every additional trial, and the odds against doubling the chance expectation of hits in 100 throws is already greater than a million to one. Professor George Temple, F.R.S., tells me that the odds against scoring—with a 20 percent, chance—400 hits out of 10,000 throws is greater than 10 followed by 500 noughts to 1 (10^{500} to 1).

Now 400 hits in 10,000 trials is approximately the score of Hubert Pearce, who averaged 8.9 hits per 25 in 11,250 trials.

If the entire human race and their descendants were to be engaged in these experiments for a billion years, it would be extremely improbable that by the end of this period, a single human being would have equaled Pearce's score, assuming that no other factor but pure chance intervened in these experiments.

The next hypothesis to be considered is deliberate fraud. Much depends on our estimate of Dr. Rhine. Now, Dr. Rhine and his wife sacrificed a promising career in biology to devote themselves to psychical research. "Their action," writes Professor William McDougall,

> seemed to me magnificently rash. The Rhines are no monied amateurs. They are working scientists without worldly resources other than their earnings. I found J.B. Rhine to be a ruthless seeker after truth, almost, I may say, a fanatical devotee of science, a radical believer in the adequacy of its methods and in their unlimited possibilities. . . . Is it not possible that his collaborators have deceived or tricked him, perhaps with the benevolent desire to reward with positive results so earnest a seeker? My reply is that, if the experiments involved only some two or three collaborators and that during a brief period only, neither Dr. Rhine nor I could perhaps adduce any completely convincing objection to such an interpretation; but in view of the considerable number of participants, often unknown to each other, and of the prolonged period of participation (extending in some cases through several years) it becomes wildly improbable that

any such conspiracy of deception can have been successfully maintained throughout and under the constant variation of conditions, without any trace or indication of it coming to light.

Dr. Rhine selected his "percipients" after preliminary tests among his students, rejecting those who did not show a notably better-than-chance record of successful hits.

The experiments varied in scope and in character and were designed to test for both telepathy and clairvoyance. If the experimenter selects cards from a pack and *looks* at them and the percipient in another room attempts to record the cards looked at, we have an experiment in *telepathy*. If the percipient attempts to name a card before either the experimenter or the percipient has seen it, we have an experiment in *clairvoyance*. The distinction is, as we shall see, of great importance in the interpretation of spiritist phenomena. In the case of telepathy, the percipient is attempting to read the mental processes of another person. In clairvoyance, he is attempting to discover, by extrasensory perception, knowledge unknown to any living person.

Experiments both in telepathy and in clairvoyance were carried out at varying distances. In some cases, the agent and the percipient were in different houses. With one exception, all those who were proved to possess extrasensory perception (ESP) were equally successful in telepathic and in clairvoyant experiments. One of the most remarkable facts is that clairvoyant and telepathic results were usually better at moderate distances, as, for instance, 100 yards, than at close range.

If these results are to be reconciled with a purely materialistic philosophy, we have to postulate a wave theory, the radiation of extremely short and penetrative waves, emitted by the agent and intercepted by the brain of the percipient. Furthermore, to cover the case of clairvoyance, the rays would have to originate, not only in the agent's brain, but also in the cards. In many experiments, the cards were not turned face up by the agent until the top twenty of the pack had been called by the percipient. This should produce an inextricable jumble of waves, if each of the twenty-five cards is assumed to emit waves to the brain of the percipient. In some experiments, the percipient has selected the right card from twenty-five cards lying on a table 250 yards away, with hundreds of similar cards "radiating" from adjoining rooms much nearer to the percipient than the card called.

But the fatal objection to the wave theory is that results often improve with distance, whereas the effect of all other waves known to physics varies inversely with the square of the distance.

I do not claim that the proof of extrasensory perception, which these experiments have yielded, definitely refutes materialism, but I do claim that it is extremely difficult to suggest a purely materialistic explanation of ESP.

These experiments have been repeated in England. According to Dr. S.G. Soal (*Spectator*, January 5, 1945), the experimental evidence for extrasensory perception "has of recent years grown to such an extent that a psychologist who deliberately ignores it labels himself as belonging to a past generation." Dr. C.D. Broad, writing in *Philosophy* (November 1944), insists that Dr. Soal's papers "provide evidence which is statistically overwhelming for the occurrence not only of telepathy but also of precognition."

Neither Dr. Rhine nor his colleagues were prepared to entertain the spiritist hypothesis. If the spirits cooperated in obtaining these results, they cooperated without the knowledge of those who carried through these experiments.

To the student of spiritist phenomena, the Rhine experiments are of critical importance. Dr. Rhine has proved that certain people possess the faculty of correctly naming cards that *no human being* has seen. Why, then, need we postulate a discarnate spirit to explain the fact that mediums in trance disclose information unknown even to the sitter and subsequently proved to be correct? If those who make no claim to be in touch with the departed dead can be proved to possess clairvoyant gifts, why should we accept clairvoyance as evidence of communication with the dead?

The value of a hypothesis varies directly with the number of facts it explains and varies inversely with the number of facts it leaves unexplained. At the outset of our search for a hypothesis to explain mediumistic phenomena, let us summarize the facts that this hypothesis must explain.

1. If we were able to keep a complete record of all mediumistic phenomena, we would find that the proportion of "hits," that is, of statements alleged to emanate from the dead which have evidential value, to the "misses," which have no evidential value, is very small.

2. In the case of the better mediums, the proportion of hits is larger than we would expect on the theory of chances.

3. The "hits" scored by the best mediums provide no information that could not have been obtained by "extrasensory perception."

4. Communicating spirits frequently become fatuous when crossexamined as to identity. "Phinuit," the spirit control of the famous American medium Mrs. Piper, claimed to be the spirit of a French doctor. He startled sitters by the accuracy of his knowledge of their past histories, but when one sitter began to talk to him in French, there was an embarrassed silence and eventually Dr. Phinuit explained that he had had so many English patients during his earthbound existence that he had entirely forgotten his native language.

5. The "Gordon Davis" case raises further difficulties for those who accept the spiritist hypothesis. Dr. S.G. Soal established contact with Davis through a medium, and the medium dramatized his personality with great success, providing unmistakable proof of identity, recalling conversations in the past between Soal and his friend, and facts in Davis's past life. The evidence for Davis's survival was

very reassuring to his friend, but less reassuring than the subsequent discovery that Davis, whom Soal believed to have been killed in the war, was actually very much alive. Davis, at the time of these séances, had made no attempt to communicate with his old school friend, either normally or telepathically and was completely uninterested in psychical research.

The result achieved by the medium can be explained by pure telepathy, tapping the mind and memories of the sitter, S.G. Soal, but if we assume that the medium succeeded in establishing telepathic contact with Gordon Davis, and in communicating some of his thoughts without Davis's being aware of the fact that his mind was being tapped, we must allow for the possibility, however remote, that a medium could tap the earth memories of a discarnate spirit. In other words, even if it could be proved that mediums got into touch with the dead, it would not be necessary to assume that the dead were consciously communicating. This hypothesis would explain the contrast between the apparent success of mediums in recalling facts in the past lives of the dead and the complete failure of all attempts to produce a plausible representation of life in the next world.

6. There is a curious dreamlike quality about all spiritist descriptions of the next world—Vale Owen's, for instance. Spirits, according to Vale Owen, do not eat and yet grow fruit trees. Spirits do not feel cold, and yet they wear clothes. They travel by an effort of will, and yet sometimes "add mechanical appliances for the sake of variety."

7. Discarnate spirits deteriorate mentally. No messages purporting to come from dead writers are within measurable distance of their best work when alive.

8. Spirit messages seem to echo the wishes of those who consult them. Good people receive edifying injunctions to morality, but those in search of less exacting sexual codes than, say, the Christian, have no difficulty in finding "spiritual directors" in the next world who are only too ready to provide the kind of advice they need.

The spirits are always anxious to gratify the wishful thinker.

When George Mallory and Andrew Irvine were lost on Everest, mountaineers would have been happy to believe that they reached the summit before being killed. I pointed out to Sir Oliver Lodge that the facts were unknown to living men and that if a subsequent Everest expedition were to confirm the accuracy of a spirit account of the last hours of Mallory and Irvine, the skeptics would not be able to explain away the coincidence by the formula "telepathy between the living." Sir Oliver sent me a long script purporting to come from Andrew Irvine. It was completely unconvincing. Many mediums busied themselves with this problem. One and all agreed that Mallory and Irvine reached the summit, but new evidence acquired in the course of a recent expedition is almost conclusive against this possibility.

Because it was pleasanter to believe that Mallory and Irvine had climbed Everest before they were killed, the spirits assured us that they had succeeded. Because it was pleasanter to believe that Hitler would not make war, the spirits continued to the last to prophesy peace. Shortly after the outbreak of the war, I read a melancholy editorial in one of the spiritist papers. The writer conceded sadly that the spirit guides had, without exception, insisted that there would be no war.

Now, there is no reason why discarnate spirits should be able to foretell the future with unfailing accuracy or why the existence of stupid and ill-informed spirits should cause us any particular surprise, but it is a little disconcerting to find that the proportion of the ill-informed mounts so rapidly once we have crossed the barrier between this world and the next. Many people believed in 1939 that war was inevitable and made their plans on that assumption. I did for one. Very few people believed, as *all* the spirit guides believed, that war would certainly be avoided.

9. The contradictory statements made about the other world, which vary from medium to medium, from decade to decade, and from country to country suggest that these revelations are nothing more than the reflections of the medium's own views and, perhaps, the expression of the subliminal consciousness.

The four principal hypotheses that have been advanced to explain mediumistic phenomena are as follows:

1. There is nothing to explain—a hypothesis popular with old-fashioned skeptics who are uninterested in facts that conflict with their preconceptions.

2. The spiritist hypothesis that it is possible to communicate with the discarnate spirits of the departed: I cannot reconcile this hypothesis with 4, 5, 7, 8 and 9 of the above considerations.

3. All mediumistic phenomena, including the "materializations" that have been witnessed under exacting test conditions, are due to unknown natural forces that the science of the future will explain. This is one of those hypotheses which can be neither proved nor disproved. It is in no sense an explanation. On the contrary, it is the equivalent of the parliamentary formula, "I must have notice of that question," and it represents an attempt to defer the answer to the remote future.

4. A small residuum of supernatural phenomena is due to the agency of nonhuman spirits who masquerade as the spirits of the dead. They possess a telepathic power that enables them to read some of our thoughts and perhaps to tap the earthbound memories of the dead. They seek, as the great American philosopher William James suggested, to prolong their social opportunities by making themselves agreeable and plausible. They weave stray scraps of information into their presentment, but they betray their mental inferiority by failure to weave them into any important or significant story.

Many years ago, Sir Arthur Conan Doyle and I had a sitting with a famous medium, Evan Powell, in private life a Welsh coal miner. During the sitting, which I have described in my book *Come What May*, we witnessed,

under fair test conditions, partial materialization, tele-
kinesis, and the "direct voice." Before the sitting began,
the sitters and the medium had tea together. Somebody
referred to one of my books, and Sir Gilbert Parker, the
novelist, remarked that his only psychic experience was
finding his room full of lights during a recent illness. Both
these little scraps of information were worked into the
seance by "Great Hawk," the Indian Chief, who acted as
Powell's "control" on the other side. He addressed me as
"Chief push-pen" and ignored my efforts to be described as
"Chief push-typewriter" and subsequently worked in the
"psychic lights." Great Hawk's voice was merely a variant of
Evan Powell's but suddenly the room was filled with other
voices. "Do you remember those psychic lights, my dear?"
said a woman's voice to Sir Gilbert, whose wife had died
a few months before. He told me after the seance that he
did not recognize the voice as his wife's.

The "direct voice," that is, a voice unmistakably different from that of the medium, is one of the few psychic phenomena that, if fraudulent, are more difficult in
the dark, for a ventriloquist can produce no effect in the
dark, a fact that the reader can test for himself by firmly
shutting his eyes next time he is present during a perfor-
mance by a ventriloquist. Shortly before the end of the
seance, I heard a whisper in front of me. "It's horrible, it's
horrible." "Don't be afraid," said one of the sitters to the
"spirit," "you've nothing to be afraid of. We're here to help
you." "You haven't heard him properly," said Sir Arthur,

"the word is 'Horace,' not 'horrible.' I knew a Horace once," and the entity "anxious," in William James's words, "to prolong its social opportunities by making itself agreeable" moved over in Sir Arthur's direction, and "horrible" became "Horace."

Thanks to my friendship with Sir Oliver Lodge and Sir Arthur Conan Doyle, I was able to secure sittings with the best-known mediums of the day, such as Mrs. Leonard and Evan Powell. Though I had no definite religious beliefs at the time, I was prepared to accept convincing evidence of survival and of communication with the dead, but I remained obstinately unconvinced that spirit communication had, in fact, been proved. I put my views on record in *Things That Have Puzzled Me* (1927) and *The Flight from Reason* (1931). My rejection of spiritism was antedated and was therefore wholly uninfluenced by my present religious convictions.

Though I did not believe, at the time of these experiments, in the deity of our Lord, I was unimpressed by the theory that the miracles recorded in the Gospels differed only in degree but not in kind from the more remarkable of modern psychic phenomena. I have already drawn attention (chapter 4) to the contrast between the miracles attributed to our Lord in the Gospels and in the apocryphal Gospels, but the contrast between genuine miracles and seance-room prodigies is even more striking. Beauty is as characteristic of genuine miracles as futility and ugliness are of the psychical phenomena of the seance room. The reader should examine the photographs of "materializations" in the works of Schrenk-Notzing, Geley, or Richet. Ectoplasm seems to obey a law that compels it to materialize in futile, foolish, or repellent forms. Most of these ectoplasmic "faces" are as vacant of expression as the face of an idiot. Almost all are repulsively ugly, and some are terrifying in their suggestion of evil. If spirits are responsible for these manifestations, we may be sure that they are unclean spirits.

In all the records of spiritism, there is no authenticated case of the cure of an organic disease, nothing to set beside the miracles recorded in the Gospels or the miracles witnessed at Lourdes. And, of course, there is absolutely nothing that lends the slightest support to the theory that the Resurrection was nothing more than a psychic phenomenon, comparable to those witnessed in the seance room. Let us never forget that the Resurrection must not be considered in isolation. It must not be divorced from its context, our Lord's *claim* to be God, his repeated *prediction* that he would prove that claim by rising from the dead, and the *fulfillment* of that prediction.

If Jesus Christ were not what he claimed to be, if he was nothing more than a deluded fanatic with unusual psychic powers, is it conceivable that God would have endorsed a false claim to divinity by the supreme miracle of the Resurrection?

Conclusion

PROBABILITY, AS BISHOP BUTLER REMARKED, is the guide of life. The overwhelming majority of our decisions are based not on demonstrable certainties but on an estimate of probabilities. Judges, for instance, often remind juries that they should find the prisoner guilty if his guilt has been established "beyond all *reasonable* doubt," and they distinguish between "beyond all *reasonable* doubt" and "beyond *all possible* doubt." If, for instance, Bill Sykes is stopped by a policeman within a hundred yards of a house, subsequently proved to have been burgled, and if Sykes' bag contains jewelry subsequently identified as the jewelry missing from the burgled house, the prosecution would not be expected to demonstrate the physical and logical impossibility of Sykes' defense that the bag had been dropped by the real burglar, who had taken fright and run, and that Sykes had picked it up with a view to taking it to the nearest police station. Sykes would be convicted in spite of the fact that no *coercive* disproof of his story was practicable. He would be convicted because on the balance of probabilities, the case for the prosecution was incomparably more plausible than the case for the defense.

The Christian explanation of the empty tomb is supported by evidence and confirmed by the cumulative testimony of events, whereas the various alternatives, which we have discussed in previous chapters, rest on nothing more substantial than the anti-miraculist dogma and the implied premise that any explanation, however improbable, that does not involve a miracle is necessarily to be preferred to the acceptance of a miracle.

The real difficulty of the Christian apologist is not the inadequacy of the evidence but the invincible prejudice that no evidence can overcome. If resurrections from the dead were infrequent, but nonetheless universally admitted phenomena, no historian would dare to dispute the evidence for the Resurrection of Jesus Christ.

Christian apologists are too apologetic. They should insist on their opponents' defining their own beliefs, for nothing is easier than to show that whatever maybe the difficulties of the Christian position, they are trivial indeed compared with the difficulties of all rival solutions.

I remember an argument about the Resurrection with a champion of mechanistic evolution. Because he did not want to accept Christianity, he assumed that he was entitled to reject it merely because there was no completely satisfactory explanation of some minor difficulty, but his faith in Darwinism was completely unaffected by the major difficulty of reconciling a theory of slow and gradual evolution with the record of the rocks, so eloquent in their testimony to the suddenness with which the new types appear.

It is contrast and contrast only that reveals the granite strength of the Christian case. Every solution to the great riddle has its difficulties, including the agnosticism which asserts that no solution is possible, for skepticism, as William James remarks, "is not avoidance of option: it is option of a certain particular kind of risk. *Better risk loss of truth than chance of error*, that is your faith-vetoer's exact position. He is actively playing the stake as much as the believer is: he is backing the field against the religious hypothesis, just as the believer is backing the religious hypothesis against the field." "Our duty," as Plato said, "is to take whatever doctrine is best and hardest to disprove and embarking upon it as upon a raft, sail upon it through life in the midst of dangers."

It is, for instance, instructive to compare the clear light of Christian rationalism, "in whose comparison all whites are ink / Writing their own reproach,"[7] with the murky mists of rival philosophies, such as, for instance, the great heresy of the nineteenth century, the dogma of a purely

---

[7] Shakespeare, *Troilus and Cressida*, act 1, scene 1.

mechanistic mindless evolution, the belief that "natural selection," a purely negative force, is an adequate substitute for divine creative power, as if the existence of weeds in a garden could be explained by the hypothesis that the gardener had not removed them. The same anti-miraculist prejudice influenced men to reject the Resurrection and to accept Darwinism, the least rational of all rival theories of evolution. The sudden and overwhelming success of Darwinism was due, not to the positive arguments in its favor, but to the negative prejudice against the intrusion of the Creator into the work of creation—as is, indeed, admitted by leading Darwinists. The doctrine of a slow mindless evolution is irreconcilable with the geological record.

Leo Berg, a Soviet scientist working under a government slavish in its admiration of Darwin, has demolished Darwinism in his great book *Nomogenesis*. He brushes aside with contempt the appeal to the imperfections of the geological record and comments on the fact that this record "in no way displays transitional forms between phyla and classes, and, possibly, not even between orders. Thus we are ignorant of transitional forms not only between vertebrates and invertebrates, fishes and tetrapods, but even between the cartilaginous (chondrichthyes, such as sharks, etc.) and higher fishes (osteichthyes): in spite of a wonderful affinity between reptiles and birds, no transitional forms between them are known."

The evolutionist feels justified in arguing from the *absence* of fossils that the more recent forms were not in existence at a time when the earliest sedimentary rocks were deposited, but he will not allow the anti-evolutionist to draw any deductions from the *absence* of all those intermediate types that the evolutionary theory demands.

The geological record is assumed to be completely trustworthy when it tells in favor of the evolutionist and completely untrustworthy when it tells against him. "In answer to the question," wrote Huxley, "what does an impartial survey of the positively ascertained truths of palaeontology testify in relation to the common doctrines of progressive modification? . . . I reply: It negates these doctrines, for it either shows us no evidence of such modification, or demonstrates such modification as has occurred to have been very slight."

Huxley, like Berg, was impressed "by the sharpness of the lines of demarcation between the natural groups and the absence of transitional forms," but by 1857 was "feeling that some workable hypothesis must be found respecting the origin of known organic forms to replace *the untenable creation theory*." Why "untenable"? Uncongenial, no doubt, to all those who are influenced, as we all are to a greater or lesser degree, by the mental climate of the age.

"I am, however, thoroughly persuaded," wrote the great biologist Yves Delage, in 1903, "that one is or is not a transformist, not so much for motives deduced from natural history, as for motives based on personal philosophic opinions." That is, on the anti-miraculist prejudice. "If there existed some other scientific hypothesis beside that

of descent to explain the origin of species, many trans-
formists would abandon their present opinion as not being
sufficiently demonstrated. . . . If one takes *his stand upon
the exclusive ground of facts*" (italics mine, as in the preceding and following quotations) "it must be acknowledged
that the *formation of one species from another species has
not been demonstrated at all.*"

"The only statement," wrote the great biologist Reincke,
"consistent with her dignity that science can make is to say
that *she knows nothing about the origin of man.*" Professor Paul Lemoine, editor-in-chief of the 1938 edition of
the *Encyclopédie Française* (vol. 5), which corresponds in
status and prestige to our own *Encyclopedia Britannica*,
writes, "il résulte de cet exposé que la théorie de l'évolution
est impossible. Au fond malgré les apparences, personne
n'y croit plus"[8]—a gross exaggeration but worth quoting as
an example of that contrast between nineteenth-century
and twentieth-century thought to which William Ramsay
called attention. Lemoine continues, "L'évolution est une
sorte de dogme auquel les prêtres ne croient plus mais
qu'ils maintiennent pour leur peuple."[9] Spengler, author of
The Decline of the West, whose philosophy was pantheistic

---

[8] "It follows from this statement that the theory of evolution
is impossible. Despite appearances, no one believes in it
anymore."

[9] "Evolution is a sort of dogma, in which the priests no longer
believe but which they maintain for their people."

rather than theistic, writes: "Palaeontology furnishes the most conclusive refutation of Darwinism. According to the laws of probability, fossil deposits are only test samples (*Stichproben*). Each sample should therefore represent a different phase of evolution, and in this case there would be no transitional forms, no boundaries, and also no species. Instead of this we find completely stable and unchanging forms persisting through long ages, forms which have not evolved in accordance with the principle of adaptation, but appear suddenly and in their final form, and thereafter instead of evolving towards more perfect adaptation, become rarer and die out, while quite other types emerge again."

Professor D.D.S. Watson, who was the principal speaker in a recent series of broadcasts, informed a body of scientists at Cape Town that "evolution itself is accepted by zoologists not because *it has been observed to occur or can be proved by logically coherent evidence to be true, but because the only alternative, special creation, is clearly incredible.*"

The theory of evolution is evolving, for facts are stubborn things and the pressure of facts is fatal to mechanistic evolution. The Creator is being smuggled back into the evolutionary process decently disguised as "vitalism" and even special acts of creation may acquire respectability if camouflaged as "mutations."

The self-portrait of the scientist that emerges from the mythology of the nineteenth century is that of a man who obeyed Huxley's command to "sit down before fact as a little child," to be "prepared to give up every preconceived notion" and to "follow humbly wherever and to whatever abysses nature leads." And this ideal scientist is contrasted with the devout Christian who clings pathetically to "preconceived notions" long after they have been refuted by science and who accepts with uncritical faith obsolete doctrines for which there is no rational justification.

But it is, as the above quotations make clear, the evolutionist who clings to "preconceived notions" long after he has admitted that they find no support in "the exclusive ground of facts." We believe in the Resurrection because it *has* been observed to occur. Professor Watson believes in evolution in spite of the fact that "it has not been observed to occur." We maintain that Christianity can, and Professor Watson denies that evolution can, "be proved by logically coherent evidence to be true." Yves Delage remained an evolutionist in spite of the fact that he admits that evolution "has not been demonstrated at all." I would not be writing this book if I could say the same about Christianity.

If a reptile, as evolutionists believe, evolved into a bird, this process took place many millions of years ago and has left no record in the rocks, for though the parent bird has certain reptilian features, there are, as Berg insists, no transitional forms between reptiles and birds. The transformation of one species into another has never been observed by human eyes, and the evidence for such transformation is mainly negative, the difficulty of accepting any alternative theory. Miracles, on the other hand, have been observed and studied by scientific observers in the modern world. The evidence for the miracles at Lourdes is not based on negative presumptions but is positive and cumulative and has been subjected to rigorous scrutiny and exacting tests.

I can understand a man accepting *both* the miracles at Lourdes *and* evolution. Most Catholic biologists believe in evolution, and many Anglican and Protestant scientists are disposed to accept the miracles at Lourdes. What I cannot understand is how any man who professes to base his beliefs on an objective standard of evidence could possibly accept evolution and reject miracles, since the evidence for the latter is so incomparably more impressive than the evidence for the former.

The evidence for Christianity is overwhelming and cumulative, and neither begins nor ends with the Resurrection. There is a fine phrase of Tertullian's, *Christus perturbatur*, which sums up the experiences of the long centuries when "Christ was being thought" and when men were looking for the revelation that was to come. The argument from prophecy reinforces the arguments based on the contemporary evidence. Again, the arguments for the Resurrection are reinforced by the argument from experience, the experience of generation after generation of Christian men, Christians for whom the Resurrection is not an academic fact, but the central reality of their lives. Such Christians will always be a small minority, but without them no purely historical arguments would convert the world.

But let us not belittle the appeal to history, for the evidence of the Christian centuries points to one conclusion: under the influence of Christianity, good men become saints and even the worst of men do not sink to the lowest depths. We, who have seen one great country, Russia, officially repudiate Christianity, and another great country, Germany, substitute the worship of race for the worship of Christ, have less excuse than our grandfathers for believing that the hard-won gains of the Christian spirit would survive such tragic apostasy.

I have by deliberate choice confined myself in this book to the Resurrection, because there is an increasing tendency, not only among anti-Christians but also among Christians, to concentrate on other aspects of Christianity. One of the oddest things about our modern opponents is their assumption that the Resurrection is irrelevant. They can't be bothered even to attempt its refutation. Some recent remarks by Mr. Kingsley Martin in this connection are characteristic of the modern attitude. I have a friendly feeling for Kingsley Martin because he is the only editor who has paid me a handsome fee for a letter that appeared in the correspondence columns, by tradition the happy hunting ground of the great unpaid, and this quixotic act tempers the asperity of the comments I must make on certain statements of his in *The New Statesman* (May 8, 1943). "My thesis," he wrote, "was that, taken together, these writers"—Marx, Darwin, Frazer, and Freud—"offer a body of knowledge of an approach to human and philosophic problems that is not compatible with revealed religion." It is not necessary to be a Christian to realize that Kingsley Martin's deities are a little moth-eaten. "The Monism and the Darwinism," writes Spengler, "which stirred the best minds of the nineteenth century to such passion, have already become the worldview proper to country cousins."

Whereas the increasing prestige of Scholasticism, the traditional philosophy of Catholic Christianity, is reflected in the attitude of many philosophers who are neither Catholics in particular nor Christians in general, dialectical materialism (the Marxist philosophy) and the labor theory of value (Marxist economics) are taken seriously only by professional Marxists.

"Frazer presented a body of knowledge," writes Kingsley Martin, "which showed that people who had never heard of Christ fashioned for themselves religions based on the death and birth of the god, and other familiar doctrines."

"It will be noticed," as Fr. D'Arcy remarks,

> that this statement contains no argument. . . . Mr. Kingsley Martin does not seem to be aware of the criticisms to which Frazer's great work has been subjected. He does not seem to know that some Christian writers look on what he insinuates as incompatible with Christian truth to be additional

197

evidence in its favour. Let me quote a passage from an essay in *The Study of Theology*, written by the late Canon N.P. Williams: "'Critical Orthodoxy' would not deny that Catholic Christianity, with its redemptive scheme centring in the death and resurrection of a divine-human Redeemer, and including the conceptions of a Church and sacraments, conforms to a very ancient pattern which underlies ethnic religions; but they would contend that this pattern springs from, and corresponds to, the fundamental constitutions and needs of human nature, and that, consequently, so far from there being any reason why the Almighty should not have providentially shaped His final self-revelation on the lines of this pattern, there is, on the contrary, every reason why He might have been expected to do so."

"Mr. Kingsley Martin," writes Fr. D'Arcy, "places side by side the birth and death of a god in the mystery religions with the life and death of Christ on Calvary. He leaves us to understand that the two are comparable. But quite apart from the vast differences to be seen on closer inspection between the two in ideal and doctrine, there is this difference which is more than decisive. The gods of the mystery religions are figments of the imagination, whereas Christ was at least a real man who lived and died. The Christian also says that He rose from the dead. If only Mr. Kingsley Martin would come to grips with that article of the Creed instead of dipping into Frazer, his argument would be less shadowy."

It is in the hope of persuading Mr. Kingsley Martin and others to "come to grips with that article of the Creed" that I have confined myself in this book to the article which affirms that "on the third day he rose again from the dead." The attempt to discuss Christianity as if it were nothing more than one of many mystery religions is as characteristic of that nineteenth-century approach to the New Testament as it is uncharacteristic of the modern approach. There is a fine passage in Harnack in which he insists on the unique character of Christianity. "Where in the story of the human race," he writes, "did ever happen aught like this? That those who had actually taken food and drink with their Lord and Master should praise him not merely as a Revealer of God, as the Prince of Life, as the Redeemer and Judge of the world, as the living force of their own existence, that these immediate disciples should forthwith be joined by a multitude of Jews and heathen, of Greeks and barbarians, of the wise and of the simple, confessing that out of the fullness of that one Man, they were receiving grace for grace?"

Freud, the fourth of the great iconoclasts in Kingsley Martin's Pantheon, can be invoked as an ally not only against Christianity but also against—Freud. The Freudians assume that objective truth is unobtainable and that the most significant thing about a man's beliefs are not the beliefs themselves but the unconscious instincts and desires that have led him to adopt his particular brand of error. But if it be true that all that is worth learning about religion can be discovered by psychoanalyzing the religious, then clearly all that is of interest about irreligion could be discovered by psychoanalyzing the irreligious. The arguments with which the Freudian defends Freud are irrelevant. The only fact of interest about Freudianism—on the Freudian hypothesis—is the particular brand of libido that compelled Freud to formulate his particular brand of error.

Freudianism, the last and vilest of modern superstitions, is completely antirational. The Freudian is engaged in cutting off the branch on which he is sitting. His denial that truth is ascertainable by rational processes leads to the conclusion that all rational discussion of Freudianism is impossible.

Freudianism is a form of Puritanism. The essence of puritanism is the distrust of the legitimate pleasure, which is the result of gratifying the natural appetites. In the third century the Manichees attacked the pleasures of sex, of wine, and of meat. At the end of the tenth century, Manicheism reached its logical climax in the Catharist heresy, which condemned the appetite for life, praised suicide, and taught that a mother who had committed the sin of procreation might atone for her sin by murdering her child. In the sixteenth century, the appetite for beauty was condemned, and the glories of medieval glass and sculpture were destroyed by the new Manichees.

The modern Puritan attacks the appetite for God. *Fecisti nos ad te et inquietum est cor nostrum, donec requiescat in te*: "Thou hast created us for Thyself and our heart cannot rest until it rests in Thee."

A Freudian would pounce with unholy zest on this dangerous admission, and would resolve St. Augustine's confession into the conventional mosaic of unpleasant complexes. He would be far too busy analyzing St. Augustine's longing for God to waste time considering the possibility that God might exist. The one common characteristic of the neo-Puritans is a resolute distaste for the examination of evidence. I have yet to find, in the works of this school, any evidence that they paused to examine the evidence for Christianity or have ever allowed their minds to dwell for one moment on the possibility that Christianity satisfies men because it gratifies the noblest of all the natural appetites: the appetite for truth.

It is an unquestioned assumption among neo-Puritans that a belief is necessarily false because it is consoling. Our belief in immortality is attributed to wishful thinking. Similarly the British faith in victory which survived the collapse of France was attributed by Dr. Goebbels to the same "wishful thinking," as if the fact that we drew consolation from our belief in ultimate victory necessarily proved that this belief had no rational justification.

To argue that the hunger for God disproves the existence of God is as irrational as to maintain that the belief in the existence of cows is an example of "wish fulfillment" because the thought of beef makes a hungry man's mouth water.

"Courage," writes Mr. H.R. Knickerbocker, "is a more important quality than intelligence. I remember I once had a spirited argument on this point with Henri Bernstein, the French playwright. Bernstein insisted that intelligence was the most valuable quality a man could have, and with enough of it he would not need more than a minimum of courage. I argued that without courage the keenest intelligence is useless in a world of action." And not only in the world of action, but also in the world of thought. Courage is tested by adherence to a creed, the evidence for which is not coercive and which appeals to rational inferences rather than to emotion. God does not coerce faith. He could provide his ministers on earth with coercive credentials, miracles so frequent and so public that none could deny them. Even Modernists might be shaken if every Christian in the London hospitals was instantaneously cured after a special service of intercession.

The conflict between supernaturalism and materialism is a conflict between reason and emotion. It is often (and falsely) said of free will that all argument is against it, and all experience is for it. Certainly all argument is against materialism, and ordinary experience lends support to it. "The world is too much with us, late and soon," the material world whose impact on our senses and our emotions at times seems irresistible. To the ordinary Christian, God is a belief; to the saint, a lover. The saint walks by sight, but the rest of us stumble along as best we may through the blackout of this world.

Francis Thomson, poet and mystic, saw—

> *The traffic of Jacob's ladder*
> *Pitched between heaven and Charing Cross*

but the only traffic I have seen between Charing Cross and heaven was the traffic of German bombers.

> *The angels keep their ancient places*
> *Turn but a stone and you start a wing*
> *'Tis ye, 'tis your estranged faces*
> *That miss the many-splendoured thing.*

But we, who are neither saints nor poets, are not necessarily "estranged" because we miss the "many-splendoured thing." This direct vision is only for the few. It is only the privileged minority who have the chance to witness a miracle or to entertain an angel unawares. But God, who is the God not only of the saints but also of the sinners, not only of the learned but also of the simple, has made it very easy for men of goodwill to discover those truths which he proposes for our acceptance—easy, that is, for those who are not so impressed by what Burke calls "the solemn plausibilities of the world" that they cannot discern the splendid certainties of the world to come.

Most of us, when we "turn a stone," are more likely to startle a slug than "to start a wing," but the evidence for the "many-splendoured thing" is no less persuasive because it is inferred rather than seen, because the appeal is to the mind and reason rather than to the emotions and senses. The Christian explanation of events is always the simple and obvious explanation. Only very clever men could concoct or appreciate the ingenious explanations of the empty tomb that we find in the works of learned unbelievers, but the greatest of intellects and the simplest of God's children have found it equally easy to accept the truths that God became man to proclaim.

Crucifixus etiam pro nobis sub Pontio Pilato.
Passus et sepultus est. Et resurrexit
tertia die secundum Scripturas.

Notes and Translations

Dedication

The poem is by Ausonius, the fourth-century poet of the transition from paganism to Christianity, for he was born a pagan and died a Christian. Here is Helen Waddell's exquisite translation from *Mediaeval Latin Lyrics*:

Love, let us live as we have lived, nor lose
The little names that were the first night's grace,
And never come the day that sees us old,
I still your lad, and you my little lass.
Let me be older than old Nestor's years,
And you the Sibyl, if we heed it not.
What should we know, we two, of ripe old age?
We'll have its richness, and the years forgot.

Introduction: Public School Religion

"Two things I may mention," writes the Rev. E.C.E. Owen, in the *Public School Religion* (p. 177), "from my experience at Harrow twenty years ago or so which suggests that boys can be interested in it [dogmatic teaching]. In those days the Epistles of St. Paul were read with very great care by the classical upper and lower sixth, that is, by about sixty to seventy boys (out of 600). I never taught them, but I looked over their papers on several occasions. They were astonishingly well done. I remember once giving full marks to a paper on the Galatians. Perhaps a colleague was right in saying that no one should get full marks for a paper on the Galatians, but it was remarkably thoughtful and thorough, and it was only the best of a good lot.

"The second incident is more intimate. There existed in one of the houses a small society of five or six boys who read papers on, and discussed, the Christian Faith; they asked me to join them, so I can say with certainty that their interests were religious in the strictest sense. They were all in one house and were friends. There is no reason to believe that their house was peculiar. . . . There may have been at the time, say, fifty boys with a serious interest in Christian beliefs, and there would be a larger number less profoundly concerned with them, but still concerned. Few branches of learning could have commanded a larger body of interested students than this."

Chapter 1: Miracles

A Catholic would define a miracle "as an event above, or contrary to, or exceeding nature which is explicable only as the direct act of God." The supernormal phenomena of the seance room would not be recognized by Catholics as genuine miracles because they attribute them not to God but to demoniacal agencies. Miracles, writes Msgr. R.A. Knox, in the C.T.S. pamphlet from which I have already quoted, "are a message addressed from God to Man. And although they may have various secondary purposes—the relief of human pain, the satisfaction of human needs, the vindication of innocence against justice, and so on—they have all one primary purpose, and that is to be an evidence—if the word had not become vulgarized in our day, I would say an advertisement—of His Almighty Power. . . . I do not even feel certain that a miracle might not be done to attest the message of some Salvation Army Missionary in China, while he was preaching all the faith he knew to men who had no chance of hearing about the faith from Catholic teachers."

A miracle is *above nature* when it involves something that surpasses the forces of nature, as, for example, the restoration to life of a dead person. It is *contrary to nature* when the effect produced is contrary to that which should have occurred according to natural law: for example, the Three Children unhurt and untouched by fire in the furnace (Dan. 3.19-30). A miracle *exceeds nature* when it surpasses the forces of nature relatively, as regards their mode of operation. Most supernatural cures are of this class, for it is often only the time factor that differentiates such cures from cures that could be effected without miracles.

Chapter 1: Marie Lemarchand

The facts are given in *Lourdes: A History of Its Apparitions and Cures* (Kegan Paul, Trench, Trubner and Co., Ltd.) by Georges Bertrin. They are as follows:

I have already described the cure and Zola's first reactions. Marie Lemarchand's doctor, Dr. La Naelle, who had been some time attached to the infirmary at Caen, when he saw how completely his young patient had been transformed, wrote: "I am still much touched by having come into contact with this absolutely supernatural cure. Marie Lemarchand undoubtedly suffered from advanced tuberculosis, and now I find no trace of it."

Bertrin describes a lecture given by Dr. Boissarie in November 1893. Marie Lemarchand was present. The lecturer read Zola's description of her appearance before the cure. "The sight of the girl's sweet and innocent face after the revolting picture which had been drawn made the people applaud loudly. Not the slightest disfiguring trace was left of the horrible disease which had disfigured the girl only fifteen months ago." In January 1904, Marie Lemarchand's doctor wrote a letter to a celebrated doctor who asked for his views. He described the terrible appearance of Marie Lemarchand before her journey to Lourdes. "She had ulcers on the face which were as large as one's hand, and which suppurated freely. . . . I saw the invalid *immediately on her return*. I did not recognize her, so much was she changed. I saw a graceful young girl coming towards me *instead* of the mass of humanity with a horrible and monstrous face which I had seen ten days previously. The tuberculosis had also disappeared. The cure had *lasted*."

Marie had been cured in August 1892. On December 1, 1905, she wrote to M. Bertrin as follows: "The dreadful disease of which I was cured at Lourdes has never reappeared. I am a housekeeper in a château. I have been married six years, have had four healthy children, and am expecting a fifth. This is what the Blessed Virgin has done for a poor invalid who was given up by her doctors and declared incurable, and was only expecting death," and she reaffirmed the fact that the cure was instantaneous "not, after several baths, but after one only."

Chapter 2: J.B.S. Haldane and Peter De Rudder

Prof. J.B.S. Haldane, F.R.S., recently stated that whereas, when he and I collaborated in our book, he was of the opinion that the odds were that De Rudder's bones were united suddenly, and that this—in his view—was more probable than the only remaining alternative, a pious fraud, his views had changed since the Spanish war. He regarded the Catholic organization in Spain as a fountain of lies, and he was now of the opinion that a pious fraud was the more probable alternative.

Prof. J.B.S. Haldane, who has been closely associated with the *Daily Worker*, feels very strongly about tendentious propaganda, but I cannot see the relevance between the alleged inaccuracies of war propaganda, on one side or the other in a civil war, and the *bona fides* of those who certified to the cure of De Rudder.

The cure took place on April 7, 1875. On April 15, 1875, fourteen parishioners of De Rudder's home town, Jobbeke, including Senator Viscount de Bus, who had never believed in miracles, and M.P. Sorge, a freethinker, signed a document to the effect that "every recourse of surgery having been exhausted, the patient was given up and declared incurable by the doctors and considered as such by all who knew him; that he invoked our Lady of Lourdes, venerated at Oostaker, and that he returned cured and without crutches, so that he can do any kind of work as before his accident. We declare that this sudden and admirable cure took place on April 7th, 1875." The statement was signed by fourteen witnesses. The document being sealed with the municipal seal, was dated April 15, 1875 (a week after the cure). De Rudder was examined by Dr. Affenaer on the day after the cure. On April 9, Dr. Van Hoestenberghe examined De Rudder and was converted from skepticism to Christianity by the clear evidence of a miracle.

Peter De Rudder's bones were exhumed after his death. "The left leg shows evident traces of the double fracture, and is repaired in such a way that, in spite of the deviation of the superior portion of the bones, which were drawn backwards during eight years by the flexor muscles of the thigh, the vertical axis of the left limb keeps the same direction as the axis of the right leg. Thus, the weight of the body was equally and normally borne by both sides. Moreover, notwithstanding the elimination of an osseus fragment from the broken limb, the two limbs are of equal length" (Bertrin, p. 181).

It is sometimes asked why, if these miracles occurred, Catholic doctors do not send all their patients to Lourdes. The proportion of cures is extremely small, and a Catholic who had no conviction that he would be the recipient of one of these rare supernatural favors might hesitate to face the journey on the off chance of a cure.

Let me reaffirm the fact that it is possible to believe that genuine miracles occur at Lourdes and yet reject the Catholic interpretation, and it is possible to be a Catholic and reject the evidence for the miracles, possible at least in this sense that it is not *de fide* for a Catholic to believe in any of these miracles.

Chapter 2: Medical Proof

The standard book on the medical aspect of the Lourdes cures is *Medical Proof of the Miraculous,* by E. Le Bec, honorary surgeon to St. Joseph's Hospital, Paris; president of the Bureau des Constatations, Lourdes. An English translation by Dom H.E. Izard, O.S.B., was published by

Harding and More, Ltd., The Ambrosden Press. Here are some extracts from his book:

Absence of convalescence. In the case of miracles, there is no period of convalescence. The subject "is cured and the injured organs are rendered capable in a moment of performing their normal functions." Had Peter De Rudder been cured by normal means, a treatment of two to three months would have been necessary before he could walk again with ease after remaining for eight years with a dis-united leg. "Some hours after the sudden consolidation of the fracture De Rudder was able to run to catch the vehicle that had come to take him to the station" (pp. 18-19).

"Clinically we are well aware of the extreme thinness of the new epidermis formed on young scars. In ulcers of the leg, for example, the surgeons are obliged to prohibit the patient's getting about too soon, otherwise the scar breaks down and the ulcer reappears. In the case of Joachine De-hant nothing of the kind happened; despite the enormous surface of the recent scar, the young epidermis of recent origin was immediately so strong that the patient could walk and undertake a fatiguing journey by rail without the wound reopening."

Cure of fracture. Fractures are cured by the formation of "callus." This callus "acquires solidity and strength by being mineralized, and this is effected by a deposit of lime which the blood furnishes to it." Pure phosphate of lime is contained in the blood only in minute quantities. "Forty to fifty days are usually necessary to form callus sufficiently thick to carry the average body weight. . . . This phosphate is derived by the blood from the food, and it is only after chemical elaboration by the digestive secretions that the blood is able to absorb this salt and carry it to the capillaries of the callus. . . . The following is the series of necessary changes through which the phosphate of lime passes before arriving at the callus of the fractured bone.

1. Introduction of food into the intestine.

2. Action of intestinal secretions and ferments upon the food.

3. Liberation of phosphate of lime.

4. Absorption of the phosphate by the blood.

5. Transportation by the blood to the cells, forming the new bone.

6. Deposition of the salts about the cells. Here we may point out all these various operations by their very nature take place successively, and this excludes instantaneity. The instantaneousness of the cure [of Peter De Rudder] constitutes the definite supernatural fact. . . .

It would be equally interesting to discover what is the unknown force which determines that this excess of phosphate shall circulate only during the time necessary for the repair of the fracture, disappearing as soon as the callus is formed (pp. 21-26).

"*The appeal to unknown natural forces* is only an evasion. To be active these natural forces should be ruled by biological laws, and these would contradict laws of the same nature. . . . Certain newly discovered forces, as, for example, electricity under the form of X-rays, Radium, and bodies of that series, have explained phenomena, the cause of which was previously unknown. They have ranged themselves alongside forces known for a long time, but they have destroyed none of them. It is quite contrary with the miraculous, which is directly opposed to natural forces. Clinical observation and physiology demonstrate to us that phosphate of lime does not exist freely in the body. It appears instantly when a fracture is consolidated. Science teaches us that the essential property of cancerous cells is to destroy the cells of other tissues and to infect their system. Suddenly they lose their destructive properties, and are replaced by cicatricial tissue cells of benign nature. The experience of centuries has demonstrated that tubercle in all lesions is extremely refractory to treatment, and a cure extends into years. Yet here at Lourdes, suddenly during a bath which lasts but a few minutes, in water which contains no agent capable of acting on the bacillus, the most advanced cases of tuberculosis are suddenly cured" (pp. 106-108).

Absence of infection at Lourdes. The town of Lourdes enjoys absolute immunity from the spread of disease in spite of the fact that there are at times more than twenty thousand patients present suffering from advanced diseases, many of them cases of virulent tuberculosis. The patients plunge into the baths, and though these are cleaned twice daily, the water inevitably contains pus from the sores and ulcers of patients. "At Lourdes are to be found accumulated all imaginable forms of infection, and only there do the people seem to have a supreme indifference for the fears of infection expressed by official hygienists." The town of Lourdes has never suffered from epidemics even during the great pilgrimages.

In Madeira, on the other hand, when wealthy consumptives began to flock there during the last century, "the native population, formerly free from tubercle, has been decimated by the scourge" (pp. 79-81).

Chapter 3: External Evidence

Other second-century witnesses to the Gospels are the *Muratorian fragment*, which most scholars place somewhere about A.D. 170, but Salmon considerably later, and which is a statement of the books of Sacred Scripture. In the fragment that survives, the "Fourth Gospel" is attributed to the disciple John.

Pantaenus's testimony to St. Matthew is convincing to those who, on other grounds, accept the traditional authorship of the First Gospel, but to cite it as independent evidence would, I think, merely provide the skeptic with a plausible object of attack.

Chapter 12: Strauss

After alluding to the various problems to be discussed, as, for instance, whether Matthew wrote in Hebrew or in Greek, Strauss continues: "Das vor Allen lässt sich unabhängig von diesen und ähnlichen Fragen erkennen, wie wir uns die evangelische Geschichte nicht vorzustellen haben. Und dieses Negative ist für unsern nicht blos historischen, überhaupt nicht rückwärts, sondern vorwärts gerichteten Zweck gerade eine—um nicht zu sagen die—Hauptsache. Es besteht aber darin, dass in der Person und dem Werke Jesu nichts Uebernatürliches, nichts von der Art gewesen ist, das nun mit dem Bleigewicht einer unverbrüchlichen, blinden Glauben heischenden Autorität auf der Menschheit liegen bleiben müsste."

"Above all, irrespective of these or similar questions, we must determine how we have *not* to represent the Gospel history to ourselves. And this negative is for us, a main point, if not to say *the* main point, for our purpose, which is not only historical, and in particular not directed backwards but forwards. It consists in this, that in the person and the work of Jesus, there was nothing supernatural, nothing of the kind which must weigh with the leaden weight of an unbreakable blind authority on mankind."

Chapter 14: Evolution

Lemoine: "It results from this summary that evolution is impossible. In truth, in spite of appearances, nobody still believes in it. Evolution is a sort of dogma in which the priests no longer believe, but which they maintain for their people."

I have written an introduction to and acted as editor for *Is Evolution Proved?*, which consists of a debate in letter form between Douglas Dewar, the leading anti-evolutionist in this country, and H.S. Shelton, a distinguished contributor to philosophic journals. My own position is agnostic. I do not think that the available evidence justifies dogmatic belief either in special creation *or* in evolution.

Buddhism and Christianity

Buddha died circa 480 B.C., but the fact that a few parallels can be drawn between a few of the sayings of Christ and of Buddha and between certain incidents in their lives does not prove that the Gospels have borrowed from Buddhist sources.

To prove this, we would have to demonstrate that these resemblances can be traced back to Buddhist literature prior to the birth of Christ, and this cannot be done. The fact is that, whereas Buddhism was unknown in the Greek world of the first century, the Gospel was carried by missionaries to India in the second century. The resemblances are therefore, in all probability, borrowed by Buddhism from Christianity, and not *vice versa*.

There is no trace of Buddhism in the archaeological and literary remains of Palestine, Egypt, and Greece, in which the primitive Church gradually evolved into the dominant religion of Europe. There is not a single ruin of a Buddhist temple or monastery in those countries, not a single translation of a Buddhist book. You may search Greek and Latin and Christian literature in vain for any hint of the existence of a Buddhist community in the Greek world. The very name of Buddha makes its first appearance in an unimportant reference in the works of

Clement of Alexandria (second century), shortly after the first Christian missionaries had reached India. Scholars such as Weber and Goblet d'Alviella, who have no bias whatever in favor of traditional Christianity, are of the opinion that the early Christian communities in India circulated the Gospel stories and that these were utilized by the Buddhist to enrich the Buddha legend, just as the more dramatic incidents in the life of Christ were incorporated by the Vishnuites into the legend of Krishna.

James Fergusson and James Burgess, in their classic book *The Cave Temples of India*, describe the fifth-century sculptures of Gospel scenes on the walls of the ruined monastery of Jamalgiri in North Panjab.

It was not until the seventh century A.D. that we find the first trace of Buddhist influence on Christian literature. The story of Buddha's conversion from the worldly life of a prince to asceticism was translated into a Christian setting by an Oriental Christian and reappears in the popular medieval story of Barlaa and Josephat.

Did Jesus Believe in the Imminence of the Second Coming?

The proportion of critics who would answer this question with an unhesitating affirmative was never very large and is now definitely less than in the first decade of the twentieth century.

The verses that lend most support to their theory are Mark 13:14-30, but it is far more reasonable to suppose that these verses predict two entirely different events, the first of which, the Fall of Jerusalem (verses 14-23), *did*, and the second of which, the Second Coming (verses 24-29), did *not* occur in the lifetime of the disciples. Verse 30—*Amen I say unto you that this generation shall not pass, until these things be done*—would be more of a difficulty if the Greek word translated "generation" necessarily refers to a *particular* generation, whereas the word can be used in a general sense for the Jewish race as a whole.

At the worst, this text is only a difficulty, and no great difficulty for those who believe in the inerrancy of Scripture. The skeptic who rejects this view has no right to assume that our Lord was reported with scientific accuracy and is not entitled to reject the possibility that the disciples may have misunderstood or misrepresented our Lord.

The dogma of *selective inerrancy* is, as I have already shown, the basis of the anti-miraculist position. Any text that creates a difficulty for a Christian *must* be accurate, and any text that creates a difficulty for the anti-miraculist is an "interpolation."

If we appeal to a consensus of the texts, of which the theme is the Second Coming, it is clear that our Lord very definitely did not encourage his disciples to believe that this was imminent. It is his wish that all Christians should be prepared for the Second Coming and should live every day *as if* the end of the world were imminent. Even in the very chapter in which Jesus is represented by the anti-miraculists as predicting the imminence of the Second

219

Coming, he assures them that only God the Father knows the day and the hour of the Second Coming. More than once he refused to satisfy the curiosity of the disciples on this point. *"It is not for you to know times or seasons"* (Acts 1:6, 7). Again, Christ predicted that "this gospel of the kingdom will be preached throughout the whole world, as a testimony to all nations" (Matt. 24:14) before the end came, and the whole known world at that time included India and China. No one could have supposed that the preaching of the Gospel throughout Europe and Asia would be achieved before "this generation" had passed away, taking "generation" in its normal sense.

The Uniqueness of Christianity

Let me conclude these notes with one of the greatest tributes ever paid to Jesus by a non-Christian:

The incomparable thing which lifted the infant Christianity out above all religions of this rich Springtime is the figure of Jesus. In all the great creations of those years there is nothing which can be set beside it. Tame and empty all the legends and holy adventures of Mithras, Attis, and Osiris must have seemed to any man reading or listening to the still recent story of Jesus' sufferings—the last journey to Jerusalem, the last anxious supper, the hours of despair in Gethsemane, and the death on the cross.

Here was no matter of philosophy. Jesus' utterances, which stayed in the memory of many of the devoted, even in old age, are those of a child in the midst of an alien, aged, and sick world. They are not sociological observations, problems, debatings. Like a quiet island of bliss was the life of these fishermen and craftsmen by the Lake of Gennesareth in the midst of the age of the great Tiberias, far from all world-history and innocent of all the doings of actuality, while round them glittered the Hellenistic towns with their theatres and temples, their refined Western Society, their noisy mob-diversions, their Roman cohorts, their Greek philosophy. When the friends and disciples of the sufferer had grown grey and his brother was president of the group in Jerusalem, they put together, from the sayings and narratives generally current in their small communities, a biography so arresting in its inward appeal that it evolved a presentation-form of its own, of which neither the Classical nor the Arabian Culture has any example—the Gospel. Christianity is the one religion in the history of the world in which the fate of a man of the immediate present has become the emblem and the central point of the whole creation.[10]

---

[10] Oswald Spengler, *The Decline of the West*, trans. C.F. Atkinson (London: George Allen and Unwin, 1926), 202.